The French Wars 1792–1815

IN THE SAME SERIES

General Editors: Eric J. Evans and P. D. King

First published 2001
by Routledge
11 New Fetter Lane, London EC4P 4EE

Simultaneously published in the USA and Canada
by Routledge
29 West 35th Street, New York, NY 10001

Routledge is an imprint of the Taylor & Francis Group

Typeset in Bembo by BC Typesetting, Bristol
Printed and bound in Great Britain by
TJ International, Padstow, Cornwall

British Library Cataloguing in Publication Data
A catalogue record for this book is available from the British Library

Library of Congress Cataloging in Publication Data
Esdaile, Charles J.
The French Wars, 1792–1815/Charles Esdaile.
p.   cm. – (Lancaster pamphlets)
Includes bibliographical references.
1. First Coalition, War of the, 1792–1797.
2. Second Coalition, War of the, 1798–1801.
3. Napoleonic Wars, 1800–1815.
4. Napoleon I, Emperor of the French, 1769–1821.
5. France – History, Military – 1789–1815.
I. Title.   II. Series.

DC220.E83 2001
944.04–dc21   2001018086

ISBN 0–415–15042–6

LANCASTER PAMPHLETS

The French Wars
1792–1815

Charles J. Esdaile

London and New York

Contents

Time charts

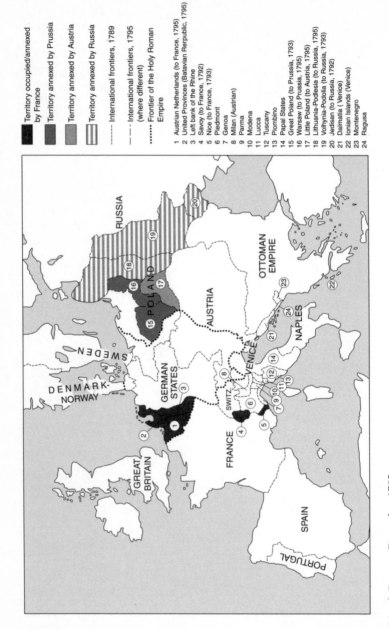

■ Territory occupied/annexed
by France

■ Territory annexed by Prussia

■ Territory annexed by Austria

▨ Territory annexed by Russia

––– International frontiers, 1789

– – – International frontiers, 1795
(where different)

·········· Frontier of the Holy Roman
Empire

1 Austrian Netherlands (to France, 1795)
2 United Provinces (Batavian Rerpublic, 1795)
3 Left bank of the Rhine
4 Savoy (to France, 1792)
5 Nice (to France, 1793)
6 Piedmont
7 Genoa
8 Milan (Austrian)
9 Parma
10 Modena
11 Lucca
12 Tuscany
13 Piombino
14 Papal States
15 Great Poland (to Prussia, 1793)
16 Warsaw (to Prussia, 1795)
17 Little Poland (to Austria, 1795)
18 Lithuania-Podolia (to Russia, 1795)
19 Volhynia-Podolia (to Russia, 1793)
20 Jedisan (to Russia, 1792)
21 Dalmatia (Venice)
22 Ionian Islands (Venice)
23 Montenegro
24 Ragusa

Map 1 Europe, December 1795

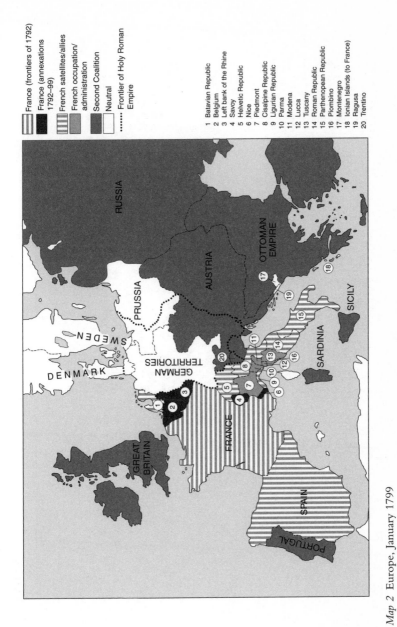

Map 2 Europe, January 1799

Source: Esdaile, Charles, *The Wars of Napoleon*, Longman, 1995. Reproduced by kind permission of Pearson Education.

France (frontiers of 1792)

France (annexations 1792–99)

French satellites/allies

French occupation/ administration

Second Coalition

Neutral

Frontier of Holy Roman Empire

1 Batavian Republic
2 Belgium
3 Left bank of the Rhine
4 Savoy
5 Helvetic Republic
6 Nice
7 Piedmont
8 Cisalpine Republic
9 Ligurian Republic
10 Parma
11 Modena
12 Lucca
13 Tuscany
14 Roman Republic
15 Parthenopean Republic
16 Piombino
17 Montenegro
18 Ionian Islands (to France)
19 Ragusa
20 Trentino

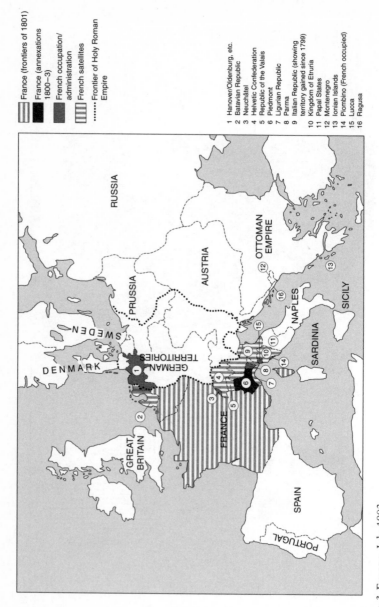

Key:
- France (frontiers of 1801)
- France (annexations 1800–3)
- French occupation/administration
- French satellites
- ········ Frontier of Holy Roman Empire

1 Hanover/Oldenburg, etc.
2 Batavian Republic
3 Neuchâtel
4 Helvetic Confederation
5 Republic of the Valais
6 Piedmont
7 Ligurian Republic
8 Parma
9 Italian Republic (showing territory gained since 1799)
10 Kingdom of Etruria
11 Papal States
12 Montenegro
13 Ionian Islands
14 Piombino (French occupied)
15 Lucca
16 Ragusa

Map 3 Europe, July 1803

Source: Esdaile, Charles, *The Wars of Napoleon*, Longman, 1995. Reproduced by kind permission of Pearson Education.

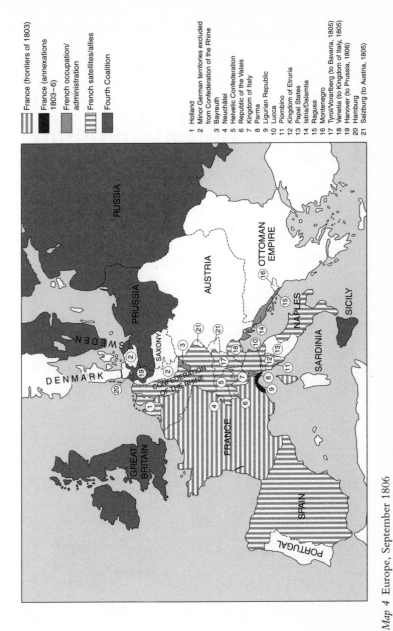

Map 4 Europe, September 1806

Source: Esdaile, Charles, *The Wars of Napoleon*, Longman, 1995. Reproduced by kind permission of Pearson Education.

Legend:

- France (frontiers of 1803)
- France (annexations 1803–6)
- French occupation/administration
- French satellites/allies
- Fourth Coalition

1 Holland
2 Minor German territories excluded from Confederation of the Rhine
3 Bayreuth
4 Neuchâtel
5 Helvetic Confederation
6 Republic of the Valais
7 Kingdom of Italy
8 Parma
9 Ligurian Republic
10 Lucca
11 Plombino
12 Kingdom of Etruria
13 Papal States
14 Istria/Dalamtia
15 Ragusa
16 Montenegro
17 Tyrol/Vorarlberg (to Bavaria, 1805)
18 Venetia (to Kingdom of Italy, 1805)
19 Hanover (to Prussia, 1806)
20 Hamburg
21 Salzburg (to Austria, 1805)

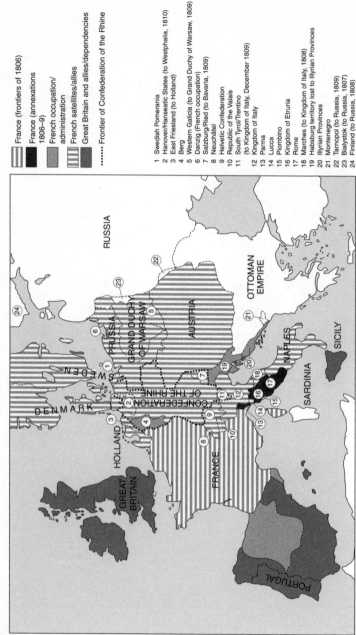

Map 5 Europe, March 1810

Source: Esdaile, Charles, *The Wars of Napoleon*, Longman, 1995. Reproduced by kind permission of Pearson Education.

Legend:

- France (frontiers of 1806)
- France (annexations 1806–9)
- French occupation/ administration
- French satellites/allies
- Great Britain and allies/dependencies
- Frontier of Confederation of the Rhine

1 Swedish Pomerania
2 Hanover/Hanseatic States (to Westphalia, 1810)
3 East Friesland (to Holland)
4 Berg
5 Western Galicia (to Grand Duchy of Warsaw, 1809)
6 Danzig (French occupation)
7 Salzburg/Ried (to Bavaria, 1809)
8 Neuchâtel
9 Helvetic Confederation
10 Republic of the Valais
11 South Tyrol/Trentino (to Kingdom of Italy, December 1809)
12 Kingdom of Italy
13 Parma
14 Lucca
15 Piombino
16 Kingdom of Etruria
17 Rome
18 Marches (to Kingdom of Italy, 1808)
19 Habsburg territory lost to Illyrian Provinces
20 Illyrian Provinces
21 Montenegro
22 Tarnopol (to Russia, 1809)
23 Bialystok (to Russia, 1807)
24 Finland (to Russia, 1808)

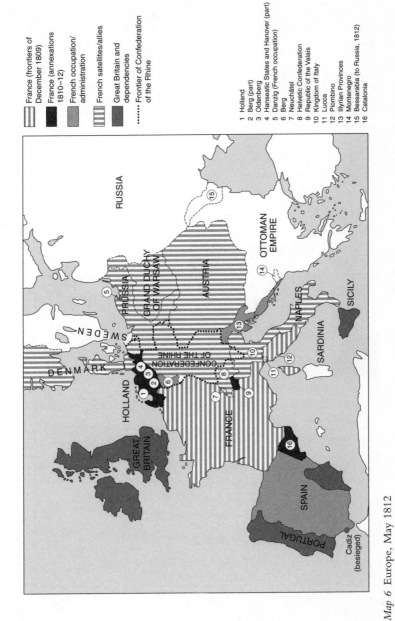

Key:

- France (frontiers of December 1809)
- France (annexations 1810–12)
- French occupation/administration
- French satellites/allies
- Great Britain and dependencies
- Frontier of Confederation of the Rhine

1 Holland
2 Berg (part)
3 Oldenberg
4 Hanseatic States and Hanover (part)
5 Danzig (French occupation)
6 Berg
7 Neuchâtel
8 Helvetic Confederation
9 Republic of the Valais
10 Kingdom of Italy
11 Lucca
12 Piombino
13 Illyrian Provinces
14 Montenegro
15 Bessarabia (to Russia, 1812)
16 Catalonia

Map 6 Europe, May 1812

Source: Esdaile, Charles, *The Wars of Napoleon*, Longman, 1995. Reproduced by kind permission of Pearson Education.

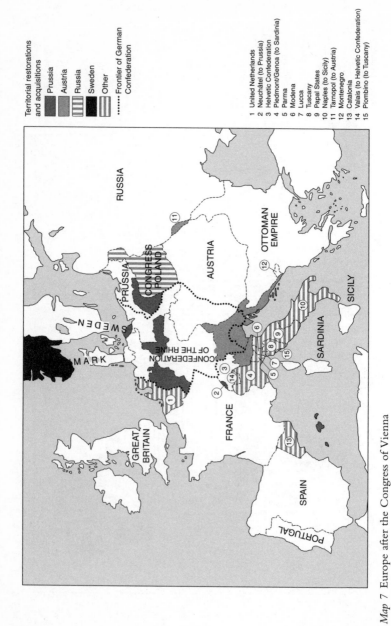

Map 7 Europe after the Congress of Vienna

Source: Esdaile, Charles, *The Wars of Napoleon*, Longman, 1995. Reproduced by kind permission of Pearson Education.

Territorial restorations and acquisitions

- Prussia
- Austria
- Russia
- Sweden
- Other
- ······· Frontier of German Confederation

1 United Netherlands
2 Neuchatel (to Prussia)
3 Helvetic Confederation
4 Piedmont/Genoa (to Sardinia)
5 Parma
6 Modena
7 Lucca
8 Tuscany
9 Papal States
10 Naples (to Sicily)
11 Tarnopol (to Austria)
12 Montenegro
13 Catalonia
14 Valais (to Helvetic Confederation)
15 Piombino (to Tuscany)

Preface

If one uses the phrase 'the great war' today, the conflict that comes to mind is invariably the First World War of 1914 to 1918. For a century before that, however, there had already been a 'great war' in the shape of the twenty-three years of bitter fighting that had racked Europe between 1792 and 1815. This struggle – in reality a series of separate conflicts bound together by the permanent enmity that divided Britain and France – had acquired immense influence. Images of its battles had been a major force in shaping expectations of what would occur should there be any renewed outbreak of general hostilities. Images of its campaigns had provided the generals of Europe with models for the operations which they themselves would have to mastermind should war break out. Images of its armies lay at the heart of contemporary theories of military organisation. Images of its passion had provided nations across Europe with fundamental features of their national myths. Images of its soldiers remained an influence in deciding how soldiers should appear, at least on parade. Finally, images of its commanders had provided generations of children with schooling in the virtues of courage and heroism.

In short, just as Admiral Nelson looked down upon London from his famous column, so the whole of Europe could be said to exist in its shadow. What, however, were the wars about? How were they fought? What factors affected their outcome? All these questions have been the subject of great debate, and yet too often the literature on the period has allowed them to become submerged in a welter of narrative. However, when they have been the centre of attention, their discussion has often, and just as inexcusably, been stripped of considerations of detail and even chronology. Still worse, indeed, discussion of the French Wars *per se* has frequently been eclipsed in favour of the consideration of other issues, a good example being the career of Napoleon Bonaparte. What is required – and, it is hoped, provided by these pages – is therefore a new synthesis that introduces them as a subject in their own right while at the same time combining analysis with narrative in such a way as not only to tell the story but also to keep in sight the significance of each event. What is not required, by contrast, is a study of revolutionary and Napoleonic Europe in all its wider social and political aspects: important as these are, considerations of space alone demand that they should be the subject of another work.

There are various people whom I should like to thank. First of all, Professor Eric Evans for being kind enough to ask me to write this work; second, Heather McCallum and Vicky Peters at Routledge for their kindness, patience and efficiency; third, my co-workers in the field of revolutionary and Napoleonic history for their encouragement, stimulation and good company; fourth, my good friends, Rory Muir, Alan Forrest, Jeremy Black and Mike Broers for their generosity with regard to this manuscript; and, lastly, Alison, Andrew, Helen, Maribel and Bernadette for, as always, their love.

Charles J. Esdaile, University of Liverpool, 15 May 2000

Time chart 1: 1792–97

1792

April
France declares war on Austria and invades the Austrian Netherlands, but is routed at Mons and Tournai. Prussia joins Austria in making war on France.

August–September
Piedmont declares war on France, the French monarchy is overthrown, and a Prussian invasion is defeated at Valmy.

September–December
France conquers the Rhineland, the Austrian Netherlands and Savoy, and invades central Germany.

1793

January–March
Following the execution of Louis XVI, the war spreads to Britain, Holland and Spain; in France revolt breaks out in the Vendée.

March–May
The French are expelled from the Austrian Netherlands and the Rhineland, while the British begin to seize France's colonial territories; meanwhile, much of France is gripped by the so-called federalist revolt.

May–August	Despite considerable success against the federalists and the formation of a radical regime in Paris under Robespierre, the Republic experiences fresh revolt at Toulon, is threatened with invasion in the Pyrenees and Flanders, and only barely contains the Vendéens.
September–December	Thanks to the *levée en masse* and other factors, the Republic first stabilises the situation both in the interior and on the frontiers, and then crushes the cause of revolt.
November–December	The Vendéen army is destroyed in a series of battles and Toulon recaptured.

1794

March–April	Poland rises in revolt against Russia and Prussia.
May–July	The French invade Catalonia, the Austrian Netherlands and the Rhineland; Robespierre is overthrown.
August–November	The Polish revolt is crushed, while the French complete the re-conquest of the Rhineland and the Austrian Netherlands.

1795

January	The French conquer Holland.
April	Prussia signs Treaty of Basel.
July	The Spaniards sign Treaty of Basel.
October	France annexes Belgium.
November	The Directory takes over as government of France.

1796

April–May	The French invade northern Italy under Napoleon Bonaparte and establish Batavian Republic in Holland.

June–September	While Napoleon continues to win victories in Italy, a French invasion of Germany is defeated.
October	Spain declares war on Britain.
November–December	Napoleon wins further victories in Italy.

1797

January–February	Napoleon completes conquest of northern Italy.
April	Austria agrees an armistice.

1

The War of the First Coalition

On 20 April 1792 France declared war on Austria; thus began a series of conflicts that for the next twenty-three years were to convulse the whole of Europe. Observers of almost every persuasion had no hesitation in viewing these conflicts as essentially an ideological struggle in which the French Revolution clashed head-on with the *ancien régime*. However, in the wake of the publication, in particular, of Schroeder's seminal *Transformation of European Politics*, it is no longer possible to sustain so simplistic a position.

Nowhere, in fact, is this more visible than in the case of the War of the First Coalition of 1792 to 1797. According to convention, France went to war in 1792 in a bid to save the Revolution by exporting her principles to the rest of Europe. In reality, however, such an explanation is at the very least inadequate. Thus, according to Schroeder, by the 1780s Europe was threatened with an immense conflagration that stemmed from, first, the erosion of most of the constraints that had hitherto kept conflict within manageable bounds, and second, the desperate search for security that this situation provoked among most statesmen.

The inevitable crisis finally exploded on 17 August 1787, when Turkey attacked Russia in a bid to claw back earlier losses. Linked to Russia by treaty, in February 1788 Austria entered the war. Seizing an obvious opportunity to strike a blow against an ever-more dangerous neighbour, in July Sweden attacked Russia, only to be assailed in turn by Denmark. Last but not least, even though Prussia stayed neutral, she embarked upon a series of manoeuvres designed to secure her fresh territory in Poland or Germany, the Russian response being to press Austria to set about her too.

When the French Revolution broke out, Balkans and Baltic were in the grip of a conflict that was monopolising the attention of the powers. However, even had this not been the case, the events that were taking place in France were not seen as being particularly dangerous, and the various princely *émigrés* who had fled abroad therefore received little help. With France herself disposed to adopt a pacific foreign policy, the pace of events continued to be set elsewhere, most particularly in the Habsburg Empire, where growing opposition to the reformist policies of Joseph II had led to a great wave of unrest whose high point was the expulsion of the Austrians from Belgium in November 1789. Coupled with Joseph's death in February 1790, these events brought major changes. In brief, the new emperor, Leopold II, was convinced of the need to restore stability to Europe, and all the more so as he realised that Austria's position was all but hopeless: Prussia was clearly a pressing danger, while both the Tyrol and Hungary seemed poised to follow the example of Belgium. Halting or even reversing domestic reform, Leopold therefore made peace with Turkey on the basis of the status quo ante.

Wise though Leopold's move had been, it merely sowed the seeds of further trouble. Eager for territorial gain, Prussia had been exploring the possibility of an alliance with France against Austria, but now changed track and pressed Austria to join her in a war against France that would lead to a complicated series of territorial exchanges in which Prussia would expand her frontiers in Germany at the expense of Austria and Bavaria, which would be compensated in Flanders and Alsace. Still opposed to foreign adventures, Leopold would have none of this, however. Egged on by Britain, which for a variety of essentially commercial reasons wanted to put pressure on Russia, the Prussians now turned their attention to Catherine the Great. Despite Austria's defection, the empress was now in an extremely strong position, for the Swedes had withdrawn from the war, while the Turks had suffered a series of major defeats. In consequence, Russia was faced with the choice of peace on the basis of Turkey's territorial integrity, or war with Britain and Prussia. However, for Berlin the aim was not just to block Russian expansion. Pressure was also to be exerted on Russia's position in Poland, where she was empowered by treaty to maintain the archaic social and political structure that had reduced the latter to a *de facto* Russian protectorate, it being hoped that the

Poles would respond to being freed from the Russians by rewarding Prussia with Danzig (Gdansk) and Thorn (Torun).

In the event, however, the scheme fell apart, largely because political difficulties caused the British government to back out at the last moment. As a result Catherine was left free to crush the Turks and extract from them the northern coast of the Black Sea. Frustrated again, the Prussians could only turn back to Austria, and in June 1791 they opened talks aimed at securing another partition of Poland. This goal was out of the question as far as the Austrians were concerned – they were desperate to maintain Poland as a stable buffer state – but they nevertheless agreed to the Prussian advances. Thus, on 3 May 1791 Polish reformists proclaimed a new constitution that overthrew the entrenched privileges of the nobility and created a modern administration, standing army and hereditary monarchy. For Vienna, this was excellent news and the Austrians were therefore desperate to forestall the expected Russian retribution. With French support extremely doubtful, the only hope was alliance with Prussia, this having the added advantage that it would force the Prussians to accept the new Polish constitution, which was no more popular in Berlin than it was in St Petersburg.

With matters in this state, the French Revolution at last took centre stage. For reasons that were essentially geostrategic rather than ideological, Sweden, Russia and Prussia all began to press for war against France. Meanwhile, Leopold II decided to use the pretext of coercing the French into moderating their behaviour as a means of creating a concert of powers whose very existence would effectively preclude war everywhere. Seizing on the pretext provided by the imprisonment of the French royal family in June 1791, Leopold therefore called upon Europe's monarchs to take joint action to restore order.

However, Leopold's strategy miscarried. In the first place, his concert of powers was stillborn, only the Prussians agreeing to join its ranks, while in the second, France failed to submit to the threat of war which Austria and Prussia duly issued at Pillnitz on 27 August 1791. Thus, Leopold had completely misjudged the political situation. At this time France was controlled by moderate constitutional monarchists. Eager to secure their own advancement, the republican element known as the Brissotins were quick to see Pillnitz's potential, while economic difficulties and freer debate had produced growing democratisation. Meanwhile, deep-seated hostility to Austria (identified in many quarters as an incubus that had sapped France's power since 1756) and well-founded suspicions of Louis XVI had already combined with foreign and *émigré* rhetoric to produce a genuine fear of counter-revolution. Last but not least, Paris was crowded with exiles whose most fervent dream was that France would sponsor revolution elsewhere. As a result nothing was easier for the Brissotins than to cultivate a war they rightly believed would republicanise France, their willingness to do so being redoubled by the belief: first, that the *ancien régime*'s armies would flee in terror; second, that war could be restricted to Austria alone; and third, that a war would ease France's numerous economic problems.

Throughout the autumn of 1791, then, France resounded to a bellicose clamour that was not only extremely alarming to Leopold II but seemed to presage the total eclipse of Louis XVI. Further concerned by the situation in Belgium, where the restoration of Habsburg authority was being challenged not just by traditionalists who based their claims on the rights of the estates but by more radical elements who had adopted the rhetoric of the Revolution, the Austrian emperor was also convinced that a Russian attack on Poland was imminent. Anxious both to restore order in Brussels and secure Prussian support in the east, as well as under pressure from advisers who believed that Austria had as strong an interest as Prussia in territorial aggrandisement, he therefore further hardened his rhetoric and mobilised an army of 40,000 men. Even now, Leopold was clearly hoping that war could be averted and thinking primarily of the general security problem, but in fact there was no hope of a peaceful outcome. In the first place, Leopold died suddenly on 1 March 1792, being replaced by the somewhat more bellicose Francis II; in the second, the Prussians were demanding immediate action; and in the third, the Austrian demands produced both the formation of a Brissotin government and, on 20 April, a declaration of war.

If 20 April 1792 saw the outbreak of war, a number of points have to be clarified. First, there was no intention of destroying the Revolution per se, it being very clear that the Austrians and Prussians were interested primarily in territorial gains. Second, the Revolution had no enemies other than Austria and Prussia: Britain had withdrawn into isolation; the minor German states opposed a conflict; Charles IV of Spain had recently installed a new administration committed to cultivating good relations with France; Gustavus III of Sweden was out of the game, having just been fatally wounded in an anti-absolutist coup; and, while eager to egg on everyone else, Catherine the Great needed all her troops for Poland. Finally, despite their rhetoric, the Brissotins were anything but committed to an ideological

7

crusade: convinced that Prussia could be persuaded to switch sides and unwilling to risk a war with the entire Holy Roman Empire, they had confined their declaration of war to Francis as 'King of Bohemia and Hungary'.

In consequence, the war was not quite the epoch-making struggle of legend. Indeed, at first it bid fair not to be epoch-making at all, two French attempts to invade Belgium collapsing in panic and disorder. Once again, indeed, France took second place to eastern Europe. Having prepared the ground by making contact with a number of magnates who had been outraged at the increase in the power of the monarchy presaged by the constitution of 1791, on 18 May Catherine sent 100,000 Russian troops into Poland on the pretext that they were fighting 'Jacobinism'. With his forces heavily outnumbered and poorly organised, King Stanislas had little stomach for a fight, and on 24 July he surrendered, leaving the Russians to restore the old constitution.

With matters in this state, events finally hotted up on the French frontier. The French had once again been on the point of invading Belgium when the Austrians and Prussians began to move into Alsace under the Duke of Brunswick. Here they encountered the French commander, Dumouriez, at the village of Valmy on 20 September 1792. According to progressive tradition, Valmy saw the new citizen-soldiers put to flight the mercenary regulars of the *ancien régime* by a combination of revolutionary *élan* and innovative tactics. In fact the raw French soldiers – a mixture of regulars and volunteers – displayed little zeal and made use of the linear tactics characteristic of the eighteenth century. If Brunswick lost, it was simply because he decided not to fight, marching his army off the battlefield rather than risk it in an attack on a numerically stronger opponent possessed of an imposing defensive position.

Valmy's impact was enormous. Precisely as the Brissotins had planned, the war had further radicalised French politics, the monarchy having been overthrown and France declared a republic. Meanwhile, the French armies went on the offensive. In late September French forces occupied Nice, Savoy and the Rhineland. Finally, in October, Dumouriez invaded Belgium, defeating a heavily outnumbered Austrian army at Jemappes and occupying Brussels and Antwerp. Much encouraged by these successes, the constituent assembly that had been elected following the overthrow of the monarchy voted to offer assistance to all peoples who wished to recover their liberty, and to implement all the reforms undertaken since 1789 in France's conquests. At the same time, the first talk began to be heard of France expanding to her natural frontiers of the Rhine and the Alps. Last but not least, having been found guilty of treason, on 21 January 1793 Louis XVI was guillotined.

Such actions clearly could not but widen the war, though so excited had the Brissotins become that it was in fact France which usually took the initiative in doing so, declaring war on Russia, Britain, Holland, Piedmont, Tuscany, the Papal States, Naples, Spain, Portugal and the Holy Roman Empire. With the Brissotins trumpeting universal liberation, the concept of an ideological war acquired a brief moment of apparent reality, and all the more so as many of France's opponents immediately instigated a period of sharp repression. Yet almost nowhere was any interest expressed in restoring the *ancien régime*; all France's enemies continued to subordinate her defeat to traditional goals (the Prussians in particular had kept most of their forces in the east, thereby forcing Catherine to agree to a new partition of Poland which brought Prussia and Russia enormous gains); and one or two states recognised the Republic and even sought an alliance with her. Meanwhile, all was not as it seemed in the other camp either, revolutionary enthusiasm failing to rule out opportunism and traditional territorial aspirations alike.

With France engaged in a general conflict, it was abundantly clear that her armies needed powerful reinforcements. Amalgamating the volunteers with the old regular army, on 24 February the Convention therefore introduced the principle of universal conscription, as a preliminary step declaring a levy of 300,000 men. The result was uproar. Large parts of France had for various reasons been left worse off by the Revolution than before, while the peasantry had in many areas become embroiled in a variety of disputes with the bourgeoisie. As conscription had always been hated by the peasantry and was rightly deemed likely to fall most heavily upon them, there was massive unrest. In most areas this did not progress beyond draft evasion and riot, but in Brittany, Normandy, Maine, Anjou and Poitou local conditions were such as to produce a full-scale insurrection. North of the Loire this took the form of a low-level guerrilla insurgency known as the *chouannerie*, but in the area known as La Vendée a peasant army was formed which wiped out the local Republican forces, defeated every expedition sent to put it down, and repeatedly threatened the Republican stronghold of Nantes. With France in total confusion, meanwhile, her armies were ejected from Belgium and the Rhineland after serious defeats at Neerwinden and Bingen.

Thus opened the great crisis of 1793. The Revolution was actually fairly secure: the Allies were short of men, ambivalent about their aims, deeply at odds with one another and extremely cautious in their operations; meanwhile, the Vendée had no means of launching a successful offensive. However, in Paris the sense of crisis was real enough, and a group emerged which argued that the only way of saving the Revolution was to mobilise the urban lower classes who were its most reliable backers, to which end it would be necessary to introduce a programme of real social reform. This the Brissotins, who were committed liberals, would not accept, and, with the aid of the Paris crowd, they were therefore toppled at the end of May. Tired of being dictated to by Paris, large parts of the country promptly rose in revolt, the Allies in the process being handed control of the major naval base of Toulon and with it the entire Mediterranean fleet.

There followed the most radical period of the Revolution. Under the leadership of Maximilien Robespierre, the Republic decreed the famous *levée en masse*, whereby all France's manpower and resources were declared to have been conscripted for the war effort, and took the most vigorous measures to translate this into reality. In part this was done by encouragement – a more democratic constitution, cheap bread, promises of free education and healthcare, and efforts at land reform – and political mobilisation, but much use was also made of terror, anyone who transgressed against the government's measures being punished without mercy (it was at this time, too, that the guillotine claimed thousands of political prisoners of various sorts).

Alone among the continental powers, France had the capacity to equip large numbers of men at short notice. Alone, too, she had a military theory capable of handling mass armies: not only was the essential concept of dividing armies into small self-contained units known as divisions well understood, but prior to 1789 the French had been developing new tactics that were particularly suited to the raw conscripts of 1793. For these reasons, and for these reasons alone, Robespierre succeeded. Massive new armies were created, desertion fell off, and the military situation stabilised. In September the 'revolt of the provinces' was suppressed; in October the Piedmontese were cleared from Savoy and the British, Austrians and Dutch from Flanders; and in December Toulon was recaptured from the British and Spaniards, the *vendéens* crushed at Savenay, and Alsace freed following victories at Froeschwiller and Wissembourg.

To what should this shift of fortunes be attributed? Traditionally it has been argued that the French armies were much bigger than their opponents, that they were tactically superior to them, and that they were more enthusiastic and better commanded. However, individual French armies were not much bigger than before, while the numerical superiority they possessed over their opponents was not so very great; the tactics chiefly associated with the Revolution – massive columns of attack supported by clouds of skirmishers – were by no means infallible; the armies of the *ancien régime* frequently fought extremely hard and could still win victories; and the many new generals thrown up by the Revolution, if often bold and thrusting, were as capable of error as any of their opponents. The French advantages rather lay in areas that were somewhat less obvious. Because manpower was so plentiful, France's soldiers were simply more expendable than their better trained opponents. As a result, her generals could fight more frequently and employ a wider range of tactics, while her armies – which proliferated alarmingly – could manage with less baggage and be pushed much harder. Coupled with the manifold advantages of the divisional system, French armies were therefore very fast moving, the division also giving them impressive flexibility both on and off the battlefield. As the Bourbons had bequeathed the Revolution with the best artillery pieces in Europe, the French were in consequence formidable indeed.

Whatever the origins of this development, 1794 more than demonstrated the great increase in France's power. On 30 April the Spanish army blockading Perpignan was routed at Boulou and driven back across the frontier, the French promptly occupying the northern fringe of Catalonia and capturing San Sebastián. On the Italian front, too, there were significant successes, the French ejecting the Piedmontese from the Alps and advancing some way towards Genoa. However, once again, the main theatre was the Low Countries and the Rhineland. A large French army re-entered Belgium in May, defeating the Allies at Tourcoing and Fleurus (an event which precipitated the downfall of Robespierre, there no longer being any justification for his policies). In October, moreover, Belgium was formally annexed to France, the French having also reoccupied the Rhineland by the end of the year.

If the Allied performance had been lack-lustre, much of the blame must again be laid on eastern Europe. In March 1794 a revolt broke out in Poland. Much alarmed, Catherine appealed for Prussian help, Frederick William being only too glad to come to her assistance. Realising what was going on, the Austrians, too, concentrated an army on the frontier, and the unfortunate Poles were soon under attack from all sides. Fighting bravely, they were nevertheless over-whelmed, Austria, Prussia and Russia then proceeding to devour Poland altogether.

Even with these events out of the way, Prussia and Russia still did not turn on France. Frederick William was now only concerned with absorbing his gains, while Catherine, pleading bankruptcy, would only agree to providing naval support. However, of all the things needed by the Allied war effort, this was the least important, the British having quickly been able to establish naval superiority thanks to the capture of the Mediterranean fleet and the immense disruption caused by the Revolution to France's dockyards and naval officer corps. Exemplified by a major victory in the Atlantic on 1 June 1794, British control of the sea was not quite complete, but even so the French could do little to protect their commerce, or prevent the British from either establishing a strong presence in the French West Indies or occupying Corsica.

In this respect, then, 1795 opened with a real boost for the French. In early January the French poured into Holland, transformed her into the Batavian Republic and captured her entire fleet. Meanwhile, the number of France's enemies diminished dramatically, Tuscany, Prussia and Spain all making peace. In July, meanwhile, came the failure of a British attempt to land an *émigré* army at Quiberon. Admittedly the Austrians and Piedmontese remained full of fight, inflicting a series of reverses on the French, but the latter were now in a position to take the offensive – especially as Spain, which was becoming increas-ingly alarmed at the British threat to her American empire – now joined the war on her side. As France's swollen armed forces and internal difficulties made more foreign gains essential, the executive committee known as the Directory that now ruled her under the new constitution introduced in 1795 planned to attack Britain and Austria simultaneously. While a large expeditionary force was dis-patched to invade Ireland, French armies would threaten Austria by advancing across southern Germany and northern Italy. However, matters did not work out as planned. The expedition to Ireland did not set sail until December, and then was scattered by a great storm. In Germany, meanwhile, the French again expelled the Austrians from the Rhineland and penetrated deep into Bavaria, only for the Archduke Charles to chase them back across the Rhine. There in consequence remained only Italy, where command had been given to a young and comparatively unknown general named Napoleon Bonaparte, who brought to his ragged army not only military genius of the first order but an unparalleled ability to inspire its devotion. Attacking in early April, within a fortnight he had won three major victories, forced the Piedmontese to sue for peace, and obliged the Austrians to retreat to Mantua, which was promptly besieged. The Austrians fought stubbornly, but Napoleon won a series of dramatic victories against them, finding time in the process to terrify the Papal States, Parma, Modena and Naples, into concluding armistices, and to establish a new satellite state known as the Cispadane Republic.

Against this flood of victories, British successes elsewhere – the suppression of French-inspired slave insurrections in Santa Lucia, Saint Vincent, Grenada and Jamaica, and the occupation of Dutch Ceylon, Demerara, Essequibo and the Cape of Good Hope – meant very little. As 1797 dawned, moreover, things grew even worse. Although a Spanish fleet was defeated on 14 February off Cape St Vincent (Cabo no São Vicente), the Spanish entry into the war in October 1796 had completely destabilised the British position in Saint Domingue. Meanwhile, on 14–15 January yet another Austrian attempt to relieve Mantua was defeated at Rivoli, and on 3 February the fortress surrendered, whereupon Napoleon marched on Vienna. Utterly exhausted, and deeply disillusioned with the British who had given Austria little assistance and had themselves been seeking peace since the previous autumn, the Austrians surrendered. The result was the treaty of Campo Formio, whereby Belgium was surrendered to France, the Rhineland left for the adjudication of a special conference, and Lombardy ceded to the Cispadane – now Cisalpine – Republic. Austria was compensated with Salzburg and most of Venice, the rest of which went to the Cisalpine Republic along with a series of papal territories (Venice's various Greek islands, meanwhile, went to France).

Peace, of course, had not come. Hard-pressed though she was by financial difficulties, naval mutinies and domestic unrest, Britain was eventually compelled to fight on by France's determination to retain Belgium. However, setting aside the wholly theoretical assistance of Russia, she did so alone, the various minor states still at war with France all now giving up. Yet it was unlikely that her isolation would continue for long, conditions in France – economic difficulties, increasing military influence and the heavy cost of the army – tending strongly towards fresh aggression. All that was uncertain, in fact, was how a new crisis would arise.

Time chart 2: 1797–1802

1797

June–July	Napoleon establishes Ligurian and Cisalpine Republics.
October	Dutch navy defeated at Camperdown (Kamperduin); Austrians sign Treaty of Campo Formio.

1798

February–March	Republics established in Rome and Switzerland.
May	Napoleon sails for Egypt; rebellion breaks out in Ireland.
July–August	Bonaparte lands in Egypt and defeats the Turks, but loses his fleet at Aboukir (Abu Qir); last Irish army surrenders.
August–September	French invasion of Ireland defeated.
September–November	Russia and Naples join the war and attack French positions in Italy and the Mediterranean.

1799

January–February French conquer Naples and proclaim the Parthenopean Republic, but are challenged by revolt in Calabria; Napoleon marches on Palestine.

March–April Austria enters the war and inflicts repeated defeats on French forces in Italy.

May–June Parthenopean Republic collapses while revolt spreads to central Italy; French suffer further defeats in northern Italy and Switzerland; Napoleon abandons Palestine.

July–August Napoleon defeats Turks at Aboukir (Abu Qir), but decides to return to France.

August–October Anglo-Russian invasion of Holland is defeated, as is a Russian invasion of Switzerland.

October Napoleon arrives back in France and overthrows the Directory.

1800

April–June Austrians besiege and capture Genoa, but are defeated by Napoleon at Marengo.

November–December Russia breaks off relations with Britain and forms League of Armed Neutrality; Austrians defeated at Hohenlinden.

1801

February Austria signs Treaty of Lunéville.

March–August Naples makes peace; League of Armed Neutrality collapses; British liberate Egypt.

October Britain and Turkey sign preliminary peace treaties with France.

1802

March British sign Treaty of Amiens.

2

The War of the Second Coalition

As has already been noted, the settlement of 1797 was unlikely to survive for very long. If this was the case, moreover, it was not the fruit of a determination to crush the revolution on the part of the Old Order, Prussia being happy to remain on good terms with France, Austria anxious for a period of quiet, and Russia eager to make peace (now possessed of a new ruler in the person of Paul I, she was beset by financial problems and servile unrest, and concerned by the possibility of further revolt in Poland). Why, then, did war engulf Europe once again? In brief, the answer lies in the position of the Directory. Faced by a revival of both royalism and revolutionary extremism, it had only maintained its position by a series of military coups, but one effect of these had been to make the government ever more dependent on an army whose commanders had a very strong interest in making war. Having repressed the radicals meanwhile, it also had no option but to pursue an aggressive foreign policy as proof of its legitimacy.

In February 1798, then, the Directory invaded the Papal States and Switzerland, both of which were transformed into unitary republics. As if all this was not enough, Polish nationalism was encouraged; the Batavian and Cisalpine republics placed under tighter French control; and Piedmont occupied, Charles Emmanuel IV being forced to flee to Sardinia. Both Russia and Austria were disconcerted by these moves, while the former had also been much alarmed by the

17

way Campo Formio signalled a forward French policy in the Balkans, Levant and Germany alike (in brief, Venice's Aegean islands had been handed to France, while the transfer of the Rhineland to France and Salzburg to Austria implied the compensation of Prussia and Bavaria from the territories of the Church, free cities and Imperial Knights). Even then, neither Russia, nor still less Austria, wanted war, but their hands were now forced by the sudden extensioin of the war to Egypt. Since the days of the *ancien régime*, assorted Frenchmen had dreamed of acquiring Egypt, which was in theory part of the Ottoman Empire but in practice an autonomous principality. For a variety of reasons, these plans were now adopted by the new French foreign minister, Talleyrand, and Napoleon Bonaparte, who was not only dreaming of fresh glories but had become the leading figure in the French high command, and on 19 May 1798 the latter duly sailed from Toulon with an army of 36,000 men.

Before analysing the consequences of this event, however, we must first examine developments that were taking place on the other side of Europe. Ireland, as we have seen, had already figured highly in French strategy, thanks to her acquisition of an active revolutionary movement known as the United Irishmen. Initially the latter's aim had been limited to political reform, but by 1795 the heavy-handed British response had pushed it into insurrectionary republicanism. Had the French landed in 1796 as they intended, they might have found much support, but their failure to do so enabled the British authorities to disarm the country. Faced with the prospect of extermination, the Irish leaders felt that they could wait no longer. In consequence, late May and early June saw revolts in Ulster and Leinster. However, the result was a shambles. Untrained, badly armed, poorly led and completely lacking in co-ordination, by July the rebels had been destroyed. However, the 'year of liberty' was not yet over. Much too late, in early July the Directory ordered aid to be dispatched to Ireland. Nothing was achieved, however. An advanced guard landed in Connaught on 22 August and, after securing some local support, set out for Leinster in the hope of reviving the rebellion, only to be surrounded and forced to surrender at Ballinamuck. The main body being trapped by a British squadron off Donegal on 12 October, Ireland was further away from independence than ever.

While Ireland was erupting in rebellion, Bonaparte was seizing Malta, thereby provoking Paul I still further, the latter having recently declared himself the protector of the Knights of Saint John. Sailing again on 19 June, by 1 July the French army was disembarking in

Egypt. After first storming Alexandria, Napoleon marched on Cairo and on 21 July crushed the defenders' main army at the Battle of the Pyramids. However, all was far from well. For all the French general's affectations of friendliness, the populace remained extremely restive, while fresh armies began to gather in the hinterland. Worst of all, on 1 August complete disaster struck Napoleon's fleet, which was wiped out by the British Admiral Nelson in the bay of Aboukir (Abu Qir).

If this defeat did not quite cost Bonaparte the campaign, it certainly complicated his position. Thus, the Egyptian potentates were emboldened in their resistance; Syria, Tripoli and Arabia all dissuaded from listening to his attempts to persuade them to revolt; and both the Ottoman government and Russia declared war. In short, Napoleon was cut off from France, threatened by land and sea, and isolated amidst a populace whose growing hostility was inflamed to fresh heights by the news that the Sultan had proclaimed a 'holy war' against the infidels. In addition to all this, his tiny army was severely demoralised and suffering terribly from disease. Napoleon, however, was un-dismayed. Putting down a full-scale revolt in Cairo, he continued with his operations undaunted, tightening his administrative and financial grip, inflicting a heavy defeat on the new Egyptian armies at Salalieh (Es Saliya), sending a small expeditionary force to Upper Egypt, and finally marching on Palestine. Seriously delayed by Turkish resistance, on 18 March 1799 Napoleon arrived at Acre (Akko). Here, however, he was checked, the garrison having been stiffened by the arrival of a British naval squadron. For the next two months the French made desperate efforts to take the city, in the meanwhile defeating a large Turkish army near Nazareth, but at last even Bona-parte was forced to give up, the siege therefore being broken off in favour of a return to Egypt.

By early June the battered expeditionary force was back in Cairo, its only achievement having been to inflict such damage on the Turkish forces in Palestine and Syria that no offensive was now likely from that direction. However, a large Turkish army had landed at Aboukir (Abu Qir), and, even though this was quickly destroyed, the writing was plainly on the wall. With the chances of relief clearly minimal, on 17 August Napoleon therefore slipped away with a handful of close companions. On 9 October he was back in France, and by 11 November he had become her ruler. Before looking at the events which brought him to power, however, we must first examine the circumstances of his absence.

In brief, France had become embroiled in a major war. In September 1798 the Russians and the Turks attacked the Ionian islands, whose garrisons were forced to surrender one by one. Meanwhile, increasingly alarmed at France's activities in Italy, on 22 November Naples invaded the Roman Republic. Despite the fact that no support was forthcoming from Spain, whose attentions had been distracted by a British descent on Menorca which was to leave that island in their hands until 1801, the French dealt rapidly enough with this crisis: the Neapolitan army was routed at Civita Castellana and by the end of January 1799 the city of Naples was in the hands of General Championnet, who proceeded to transform the Neapolitan mainland – for Ferdinand IV had taken refuge in Sicily – into the Parthenopean Republic. By this time, a far more serious threat had emerged, however, for Austria now also entered the war. Opposed to the expansion of French influence in Italy, guaranteed Russian support in the form of a large army that had been mobilised by Paul I on his western frontier, and as certain as he could be that Prussia would remain neutral (there had been some fear that she would actually join the French, but the deployment of a Russian army in Poland had put paid to any such danger), Francis II finally decided on war, the forces that had been concentrated in Russia's western borderlands therefore being sent to join the Austrian armies.

The onset of general hostilities placed the Directory in a distinctly unfavourable position. Notwithstanding the *levée en masse*, a formal system of conscription had only been introduced into France in September 1798, with the result that her strength had fallen far below the levels of 1793–94. Moreover, conscription initially only made matters worse. Revolts broke out in the west, the south and Belgium, while draft evasion reached epic proportions. As a result, no more than 250,000 men were available, while even these were dispersed along a line that stretched from Holland to Naples. Meanwhile, though not yet exposed to conscription, the occupied territories still had plenty of grievances. The year 1798 had already witnessed serious revolts in the Helvetic Republic and Malta (where the help of the Royal Navy enabled the insurgents to confine the French to Valetta, which was blockaded), while the occupation of the city of Naples had taken place only in the face of desperate popular resistance. Almost everywhere, in short, the French were not only facing powerful regular armies, but also an angry populace.

Not surprisingly, the result was disaster: in Italy, initial success in the form of a peaceful occupation of Tuscany was offset by a massive popular revolt in Calabria and an Austro-Russian offensive in the north that gained the ferocious General Suvorov a series of victories, precipitated a further series of insurrections in Tuscany, Lombardy and Piedmont, and forced the French to evacuate all their conquests except Genoa; in Germany the French were beaten by the Austrians at Ostrach and Stockach; and in Switzerland, with the French hampered by continued guerrilla warfare, another Austro-Russian army advanced as far as Zurich.

With the precarious nature of France's satellite regimes thus made cruelly apparent, on 15 August a French counter-offensive in northern Italy was broken at Novi. However, at this point the Directory was saved by a combination of a much improved domestic situation and the political differences that erupted among its opponents. Thus, the most serious revolts that had broken out in France had been crushed and the flow of recruits greatly improved. As for relations between the Allies, the British and Russians were fighting for the restoration of the frontiers of 1789, while the Austrians wanted territorial gains in Germany and Italy. Determined, in consequence, to ensure that the Austrians had little say in an eventual peace settlement, the British and Russians settled on a strategy which gave the main emphasis to their own forces. Thus, all the Russian troops in the west were concentrated in Switzerland, from where they would invade central France, while an Anglo-Russian expeditionary force was sent to conquer Holland. However, the result was failure. In Switzerland the French struck before the planned Russian concentration had taken place, mauling the Russian force already *in situ* at Zurich on 25 September, and forcing Suvorov's corps, currently on the march from northern Italy, to engage in a nightmarish retreat that left it unfit for any further operations. Meanwhile, the Dutch campaign soon became bogged down, and was abandoned altogether after a serious defeat at Castricum on 6 October.

Although attacks in both Italy and Germany were repulsed by the Austrians at Grenola and Sinzheim, France was therefore very much back in the war when Napoleon returned home. Nevertheless, he remained the man of the moment. The crisis of 1799 had led to a Jacobin revival that the Directory seemed powerless to counter, the summer of 1799 witnessing a new *levée en masse* – to be precise, the mobilisation of five classes of conscripts at once – a forced loan and a new 'law of hostages'. Faced by this threat, a number of moderates decided that the power of the executive had to be strengthened. Revision of the constitution being all but impossible, the only way forward was a military coup, this in turn requiring a suitable general. Napoleon was not in fact the first choice of the conspirators for such a role, their attention being initially directed to rather more pliable figures, but for one reason or another these fell by the wayside, the consequence being that it was the Corsican who ended up as the figurehead.

The consequences of the subsequent coup of 18 Brumaire (10–11 November 1799) were overwhelming. As First Consul – France had been given a new constitution which invested her with a three-man collective presidency called the Consulate – Napoleon's principles were simple. Always fascinated by power, the new ruler was determined to strengthen the state. To achieve this, he used a remarkable mixture of co-option, coercion and reform. Thus, the propertied classes – noble or non-noble, Jacobin or royalist – were offered a place within the régime, a political system that gave them a monopoly of office and a code of law – the famous civic code – that guaranteed the social and economic gains they had made in the Revolution. Meanwhile, the Catholic Church was effectively incorporated into the apparatus of the state through the Concordat of 1801, and Jacobin dechristianisation abandoned. With the ground thereby cut from under the feet of much of the popular resistance which had so marked the 1790s, immense strides were made in the organisation of the state. Thus, local government in particular was reformed on a rigidly hierarchical model that made it far more responsive to the demands of Paris and reinforced by a highly effective system of coercion. Success was not immediate – there were, in fact, areas that were never fully subordinated – but the result was that France's men and money were now tapped in a fashion never equalled by the Revolution.

However, much of this was a long way in the future. As Napoleon recognised, peace was the most immediate need. Virtually the first action of Consular diplomacy was therefore the dispatch of peace feelers to Britain and Austria, but these were hardly serious. Though all was not well with the Second Coalition, Bonaparte knew perfectly well that the Austrians were strongly entrenched in Italy and Germany, and the British supreme at sea and in the colonies (over the past three years, Britain had not only won success in the Mediterranean, but shattered French influence in India). Having thrown the responsibility for continuing the war upon his enemies, the French ruler could now seek further victories that would augment his glory and allow him to dictate peace on his own terms.

There followed the campaign of 1800. Although the advantage now lay with the French – believing that his troops had been betrayed by the Austrians, and further angered by a growing British inclination to side, for pragmatic reasons, with Vienna's plans for the settlement of Italy, Paul I had withdrawn from the war – it was the Allies who took the initiative. Thus, bolstered by a much-needed British loan, the Austrians besieged Genoa. Although taken by surprise, Napoleon's response was dramatic: while Moreau defeated the Austrians at Stockach on 3 May, the First Consul crossed the Alps and descended on the Austrian rear, winning a great victory at Marengo on 14 June. Although this came too late to save Genoa, the Austrians had in consequence to evacuate their Italian conquests, while a further defeat at the hands of Moreau at Hohenlinden on 3 December led them finally to give way. The result was the Treaty of Lunéville, by which Austria was forced to accept France's annexation of Belgium and the left bank of the Rhine, recognise the independence of the satellite states, and cede Modena, together with some of the Venetian territory she had acquired in 1797, to the Cisalpine Republic. Meanwhile, to compensate Spain for ceding Louisiana to France, as she had just done, Tuscany was given to Charles IV's daughter as the Kingdom of Etruria.

With Austria completely humbled, there yet remained the Ottoman Empire, Britain, Naples and Portugal. If Britain's capture of Malta – whose garrison was forced to surrender in September – is excepted, none of these countries had played much part in the campaign of 1800, but they now found themselves bearing the brunt of the war. First to suffer was Naples which was forced to sue for peace after defeat at Siena on 14 January 1801. Next to fall was Portugal which in May 1801 was invaded by Spain and compelled to surrender. However, the British had meanwhile resolved to liberate Egypt. On 8 March 1801, 15,000 British troops therefore disembarked near Alexandria. Quickly defeating the French, they besieged that city and set off for Cairo, being reinforced *en route* by a Turkish army that had arrived from Palestine. Demoralised and outnumbered, the capital's garrison surrendered on 28 June, while on 30 August Alexandria, too, capitulated.

The capture of Alexandria was the final action of the war. Before we close, however, we must briefly look at events in the Baltic. In the course of 1800 clever manipulation by France had steadily widened the gulf between Russia and her erstwhile allies, and by the autumn Paul I was mobilising an army on the Austrian frontier, laying plans for a march on India, and organising the Baltic states into a maritime alliance against Britain – the so-called League of Armed Neutrality. For Napoleon these events were highly promising, but on 23 March 1801 Paul was murdered in a coup precipitated by his determined efforts to modernise the Russian state, while on 2 April the British defeated the Danish fleet at Copenhagen, the Armed Neutrality promptly falling apart.

Napoleon was now placed in a very difficult position. Not only was his last hope of defeating Britain gone, but it was clear that there was little hope of getting help to Egypt. If anything was to be rescued from the débâcle, a compromise settlement was essential. This would also allow him to play the peacemaker, rebuild his navy, further his programme of reform, and tighten his grip on Germany. Meanwhile, the British seemed likely to accept whatever terms they were offered since their prospects were limited. They were now devoid of allies, victory in Egypt having caused the Turks to withdraw from the war, and their domestic situation was decidedly rocky. There was a growing economic crisis; Ireland remained restive; and disputes with George III had led to the prime minister's replacement by the far less able Addington. The result was, first, the preliminaries of London (1 October 1801) and second, the Treaty of Amiens (25 March 1802). For the first time in almost ten years, the whole of Europe was at peace.

Time chart 3: 1803–6

1803

May–June   Britain declares war on France and launches an offensive in the West Indies; French troops occupy Hanover and Naples and begin to mass at Boulogne.

August–November   British overthrow Mahratha Confederacy.

1804

March   Outbreak of Serbian revolt.

October   British reopen hostilities with Spain.

December   Napoleon crowned Emperor of France.

1805

May   France annexes Ligurian Republic; Napoleon crowned King of Italy.

July–October   Britain, Russia, Austria, Naples and Sweden form Third Coalition.

October   Napoleon defeats Austrians at Ulm; French and Spaniards defeated at Trafalgar.

November	French occupy Vienna; British forces disembark in Hanover; Anglo-Russian forces land at Naples.
December	Russians defeated at Austerlitz (Slavkov); Austria signs Treaty of Pressburg (Bratislava).

1806

February	French invade Naples; British evacuate Hanover but garrison Sicily.
March	Napoleon opens peace negotiations with Britain.

3

The War of the Third Coalition

With the signature of the Treaty of Amiens, the whole of Europe was at peace for the first time in ten years. These were, however, ten years in which the balance of power had been totally transformed. No longer the second-rate power of 1792, France had considerably augmented her territory, established several satellite republics, and greatly expanded and improved her army. As for her opponents, Britain had secured complete supremacy at sea and made considerable advances in the colonies, while Austria, Prussia and Russia had all made substantial territorial gains. Thus, there loomed the possibility of fresh conflict, but Lunéville and Amiens were no more unstable than earlier settlements. Since neither Britain, nor Austria, nor Prussia nor Russia was at all eager to disturb the peace, Europe might have been granted a breathing space in other circumstances, but France was ruled by Napoleon Bonaparte and thus it was that nothing of the sort occurred.

To understand the process by which the war was resumed, it is necessary to discuss the treaty that brought the conflict of 1792 to 1802 to an end. In this respect, the chances of peace were not helped by the fact that the settlement was essentially an unequal one. In order to obtain peace, Britain offered terms that were extremely generous. France's natural frontiers and satellite republics were recognised, Menorca returned to Spain and Malta to the Knights of Saint John. Most of the French, Dutch and Spanish colonies were also restored, the sole exceptions being Trinidad and Ceylon. In return,

France had only to withdraw from all her satellites and respect their independence. Britain, in short, had gained almost nothing from nine years of war.

For the peace to hold, much would depend upon Napoleon. At the very least, the First Consul would have to withdraw his troops from Holland, Switzerland and Italy, respect Cisalpine, Ligurian, Helvetic and Batavian independence, and generally restrain his actions in the continent of Europe. A liberal policy towards British trade and prudence in the wider world would also be advisable. Given Napoleon's character, however, all this was most unlikely. Far from remaining quiet, he continued to intervene in areas bordering on his frontiers: though Naples and Switzerland were evacuated, French troops continued to occupy Holland, while in January 1803 Switzerland was reoccupied, given a new statute and stripped of the Valais; the Cisalpine (now Italian) Republic was reordered along French lines with Napoleon as its president; Piedmont and Elba were annexed; and the Holy Roman Empire was effectively dismantled. So important was this last development that it must be looked at in some detail. A heterogeneous collection of territories united only by the theoretical allegiance of their rulers to the House of Habsburg, the Empire was a major bastion of Austrian influence, and as such an object of Napoleon's ire. At the same time, however, it was also threatened from within, for its stronger members had become determined to absorb their weaker fellows. Such a policy was disastrous for Austria, whose strongest supporters in the Empire had traditionally been its weaker members, but the problem of finding some compensation for the evicted Italian Habsburgs was now attracting even Francis II to the process. Having annexed the Rhineland, the French had suggested that the German rulers affected should be compensated by the acquisition of fresh territory across the river. The Germans being unable to agree among themselves, Napoleon was effectively left to arrange a settlement. While Austria and Prussia were bought off with the Trentino and substantial territories in Westphalia, middling states such as Bavaria, Baden and Würtemberg were allowed to make huge gains. At a stroke Germany was transformed. The Holy Roman Empire survived, but its members were reduced from 365 to forty and Austria's predominance was replaced by that of France, the many middling states naturally looking to Napoleon for protection.

Needless to say, none of this was to Britain's taste, her unease being heightened by Napoleon's actions in other areas. British trade continued to be discriminated against, while French activity in the wider world showed no signs of abating. Having already dispatched an expedition to Australia, restored friendly relations with the United States (with which France had been on the brink of war), and restored slavery in the French colonies, the First Consul established friendly links with Tunis and Algiers, floated the possibility of a fresh expedition to Egypt, attempted to restore French influence in India, dispatched an army to reconquer Saint Domingue, and commenced a large programme of naval construction. In short, the British could be justified in feeling that their interests were being challenged on every side.

If few of Napoleon's actions infringed the letter of the Treaty of Amiens, they certainly infringed its spirit, while persuading London that he would soon abandon it altogether. When repeated protests failed to produce any result, the Addington administration resolved to resist France over Malta, which Britain had not yet evacuated. As a result, Napoleon was faced with demands to evacuate Holland and Switzerland, respect the satellite states' independence, and sanction British occupation of Malta for ten years. Realising that he had overplayed his hand – for France's programme of naval construction was not much advanced – Napoleon attempted to draw back, but in the last resort his pride would not let him do so sufficiently. Addington still did not want conflict – Amiens had, after all, largely been his creature – but he could see no other option, and on 18 May 1803 Britain declared war.

The next few months were curiously quiet, the fact being that neither Britain nor France could easily strike at one another. For the former the only viable move was a resumption of the blockade and a renewed offensive in the wider world – Santa Lucia, Tobago, Demerara and Essequibo had soon all been captured, the slaves assisted in the liberation of Saint Domingue and the French-backed Mahratha Confederacy shattered beyond repair. Although they were soon joined by their various satellites, the French could only respond by seizing Hanover, of which George III was the ruler, and seeking to hamper British trade, to which end they quickly occupied both the north German coast and the Neapolitan ports of Taranto, Otranto and Brindisi. Meanwhile, a heavy subsidy was extracted from Spain in exchange for her neutrality. However, Napoleon was not content with such measures, and he therefore commenced preparations for an invasion of England.

Although the invasion scheme was taken very seriously in Britain, the danger was absolutely minimal. The French fleet was scattered between half a dozen different ports, short of manpower, lacking in stores and increasingly devoid of ocean-going experience, while the invasion flotillas were slow and unseaworthy. It was also becoming obvious that Napoleon would sooner or later have other foes to deal with. In May 1803, the prospect of a wider European conflict seemed very far-fetched indeed. Unwilling to risk the prospect of fresh French victories, the British did not initially show much interest in finding allies. Eventually, however, they turned to Russia, only to find that, though Alexander I had become increasingly irritated with Napoleon, he was not interested in going to war, since his main object was to extend his influence in eastern Europe. As for Austria and Prussia, meanwhile, the former was afraid of Russia and increasingly inclined to see her future in the Balkans, and the latter was convinced that her best interests lay in continued *rapprochement* with France.

The man responsible for the formation of the Third Coalition was therefore not Pitt (who had returned as prime minister in place of Addington in 1804), but Napoleon. In this respect, much weight is often given to the kidnap and execution of the Duc d'Enghien on suspicion of involvement in a royalist conspiracy, but far more important was the threat which France posed to the balance of power. As we have seen, the war had produced an immediate expansion of French influence. For all the eastern powers, the occupation of Hanover and its fellows was both alarming and injurious: thus, Austria feared for her trade, while being deeply concerned about the growth of French preponderance in Germany and Italy; Prussia found herself menaced by a large French army and cheated of a major prize; and Russia objected both to what she perceived as renewed French interest in the Levant and the destabilisation of the settlement of Germany agreed in 1803 (in which Alexander had a personal interest given that many of the German princes were connections of the Russian royal family). However, for the time being, both Austria and Prussia remained quiescent: terrified of war – the 1790s had clearly shown that her finances simply could not cope with a major conflict – Austria was intent on making use of French preoccupation with Britain to secure concessions in Germany, while Prussia was mollified by a vigorous 'peace offensive'. Had Napoleon been placatory with regard to Russia, even she might have been conciliated, but the French ruler could not resist displaying a disturbing interest in the now-independent Ionian islands and mainland Greece. Then on 18 May 1804 came the declaration that France was henceforth a hereditary empire, the echoes of Charlemagne this carried with it suggesting that Napoleon intended to secure control of the whole of Germany. With varying degrees of enthusiasm, the tsar and his advisers consequently began to work for a new coalition that would drive Napoleon back at least to the limits agreed at Lunéville and Amiens, obtaining for this purpose the promise of substantial British subsidies. Meanwhile, an ultimatum was sent to Napoleon demanding that he evacuate Hanover and Naples, the French ruler's refusal to comply leading Russia to break off diplomatic relations in September 1804.

With a Franco-Russian rupture now a reality, it would appear that a wider conflict was inevitable. However, even now there were considerable problems: in October 1804, for example, Britain had shocked European opinion by launching a surprise attack on Spain on the grounds that she was covertly aiding France and might as well be forced to enter the war, while there were persistent fears that her intention was to embroil the other powers of Europe in the war so as to allow her to scale down her own commitment to the struggle. With quarrels also breaking out over Malta, which both Britain and Russia desired for themselves, by mid-1804 an Anglo-Russian alliance seemed to have become impossible. As for other partners, only Sweden was prepared to go to war: despite clear evidence that Napoleon was planning a new German confederation that would finally overthrow the Holy Roman Empire, the most that Austria would agree to was a defensive alliance that would come into action in the event of further French aggression in Italy or Germany; as for Prussia, fears that Napoleon might launch a surprise attack were countered by suspicions of Russia and Sweden, Frederick William's response being to assure the French ruler of his friendship and even to explore the possibility of an alliance.

At the beginning of 1805, then, the Third Coalition was really no closer than before. On 11 April Britain and Russia admittedly succeeded in negotiating an alliance that committed the latter to war unless Napoleon agreed to conform to Amiens and Lunéville, and laid down the aim of excluding the French from Holland, Switzerland and northern Italy. However, a fierce quarrel immediately developed over Malta, and the treaty remained unratified for some time. As it was also dependent on Austria, who was expected to provide most of the troops required, it was in any case null and void, for Vienna was still refusing to take part in an offensive war. However, not content

31

with restyling the Italian Republic as a kingdom with himself as ruler and his stepson Eugène de Beauharnais as viceroy, in early June Napoleon suddenly announced the annexation of Genoa – the Ligurian Republic – Parma and Piacenza, and appropriated Lucca as a principality for his younger sister Elise. The situation was immediately transformed. Britain and Russia resolved their differences and ratified the treaty of 11 April, whereupon Austria rushed to join the alliance as well. Although Francis II and his chief military adviser the Archduke Charles remained opposed to war, they could not tolerate Napoleon's actions, and feared that an attack was coming anyway. Another potential member of the coalition was Naples, but with French troops on her soil she could do no more for the time being than secretly appeal for assistance.

With war looming in the east, on 26 August 1805 the erstwhile 'Army of England' – now renamed the *grande armée* – was ordered to leave the Channel coast for the Rhine. In ordering this move, Napoleon was in all probability very relieved, for the only hope of invasion had just disappeared. In the last resort, the scheme had always depended on the French and Spanish squadrons scattered from Toulon to Brest evading the British blockade and either uniting in the West Indies, thereby forcing the Royal Navy to leave the Channel unguarded, or joining forces for a desperate struggle off the British coast itself. By the summer of 1805, however, a complex series of naval operations had shown that the chances of success were all but non-existent, the presence of the army of England at Boulogne therefore having become a considerable embarrassment.

With the invasion attempt definitively abandoned, Napoleon would have done best to leave his fleets in port. However, the emperor now needed as many troops as he could muster, and therefore ordered the large Franco-Spanish force that had gathered at Cádiz to make for Naples so as to put ashore the 4,000 troops carried by its ships. Despite the fact that his ships were unfit for battle, the French admiral Villeneuve realised that he had no option but to comply, and on 20 October he therefore put to sea. Commanded by Nelson, the British imediately closed in upon him, and the result was the Battle of Trafalgar (21 October 1805). Nelson was killed, but Villeneuve's fleet was broken beyond repair – of his thirty-three men-of-war, eighteen were lost and most of the remainder crippled.

Despite much bluster, Trafalgar led Napoleon to concentrate on defeating Britain by economic means. In the meantime, however, he was achieving great success. Faced with the prospect of a concentric attack by armies that were supposed to amount to some 500,000 men, the emperor had struck into Germany with the greatest speed, while secondary forces held off the Allies in Italy where the French had been forced to evacuate Naples in the face of an Anglo-Russian expeditionary force. Though not without its problems – shortage of horses, for example – the *grande armée* was without equal. In large part composed of veterans who had spent the years since 1801 being drilled and trained without let-up at the so-called 'camp of Boulogne', it possessed a tactical system that was much more flexible and effective than that of its continental opponents, while Napoleon had greatly improved upon the organisational model he had inherited from the Republic through the establishment of both army corps and special reserves of artillery and cavalry. The army was thus able to move very fast, operate on a broad front that facilitated envelopment, display an extraordinary level of flexibility, and hit very hard on the actual battlefield; it had also been imbued with high morale and given a group of commanders who represented the cream of revolutionary generalship. As for the Allies, meanwhile, their armies were at best still coming to terms with the changes in warfare wrought by the French Revolution, while they were also beset by difficulties of every sort, the result being that many of the expected troops either failed to appear altogether or only did so when it was much too late. Nor were matters helped by the fact that both the coalition itself and the internal counsels of some of its participants continued to be rent by major disagreements; that the Swedes, in particular, would not move unless the Prussians did so too; that the Russians reserved many of their forces for possible use in the Balkans, having been much excited by the outbreak of a revolt against the Turks in Serbia in 1804; and that the chain of command in the field was extremely muddled.

The result was chaos. Untrammelled by any significant threat to its northern flank, the *grande armée* swung smoothly across the Rhine and then headed south-eastward with the aim of defeating the army which the Austrians had massed on the Bavarian frontier under Archduke Ferdinand. Convinced that no French forces could appear until late October, by which time the Russians should have come to his assistance, Ferdinand had meanwhile invaded Bavaria, advanced to the Danube and moved westward to Ulm. To his considerable surprise, Napoleon therefore suddenly found himself to the rear of the Austrians, and hastily swung his army westward to envelop them. In the confusion, some of his prey managed to get away, but on 20 October the survivors laid down their arms.

In Italy things had gone rather better for the Austrians, but the general situation was catastrophic. Although the first Russian troops had at last arrived at the frontiers of Bavaria, they were few in number and exhausted, while close to 60,000 men had been lost at Ulm. Still worse, the French were heading straight for Vienna. By dint of hard marching, the Russians and most of the Austrian troops still in the vicinity escaped to Bohemia, but on 12 November the capital was occupied. The war, however, was not over. Thanks to the arrival of more Russians, there were now over 80,000 troops in Bohemia. Convinced that he could win a great victory, Alexander I, who had arrived from Russia, ordered an offensive, and by 1 December the two armies had gathered near the town of Austerlitz (Slavkov).

What followed was possibly the most masterly battle of the emperor's career. Enticed to attack the French right in an effort to sever Napoleon's communications with Vienna, the Allies left their centre unguarded, and this allowed the emperor effectively to split them in two. Thrown into complete disorder, they fought with great courage, but by the end of the day – the first anniversary of Napoleon's coronation – their left flank was all but surrounded and the rest of the army streaming away in varying states of disorder. All in all, their casualties amounted to some 25,000 men, while the French had suffered losses of only 8,000.

Needless to say, Austerlitz dealt a death-blow to the Third Coalition. On the brink of joining its ranks, Prussia instead hastily committed herself to an offensive–defensive alliance with Napoleon that promised her Hanover in exchange for a guarantee of France and her satellites and the cession of a number of German territories. Meanwhile, the defeat paralysed Allied operations in northern Germany and persuaded Austria, whose horrified emperor had also been at Austerlitz, to seek an immediate peace settlement even though the terms proved ruinous. By the Treaty of Pressburg (Bratislava), Austria was forced to cede Venetia, Dalmatia and Istria to the Kingdom of Italy, Vorarlberg, Tyrol and Trentino to Bavaria, and the isolated pockets of territory still held by Austria in south-west Germany to Baden and Würtemberg. In addition, Napoleon had to be accepted as King of Italy, and Bavaria, Würtemberg and Baden recognised as independent states, while Austria also had to pay an indemnity of 40 million francs. The only compensation was that Austria was allowed to regain Salzburg, the Habsburg Duke of Tuscany, to whom it had been given in 1803, receiving in exchange the Grand Duchy of Wurzburg. As for the Russians, they hastily evacuated their forces from Germany and Bohemia alike, and began to seek a separate peace.

The Allied forces in northern Germany either remained quiet or pulled out; thus the war continued in only the Mediterranean and the wider world. In the former, Naples had been occupied by the Anglo-Russian expeditionary force, which, together with the Neapolitan army, was now manning her northern frontier, but the Allies were short of supplies and increasingly at odds with one another. Realising that their position was hopeless, in January 1806 the British and Russians retired to the respective havens of Sicily and Corfu (Kerkira). Hard on their heels, nearly 40,000 French troops marched across the frontier. Left with no option but to flee, the royal family set sail for Sicily, their place being taken by Joseph Bonaparte (it was at this time, too, that Holland was transformed into a kingdom under Louis Bonaparte). In short, by mid-March the mainland of Europe was quiet. Britain continued to reign supreme at sea and in the colonies, but otherwise the picture seemed bleak indeed.

Yet all was not lost. Not only was Britain's power intact, but it had become clear that Napoleon would be able to strike at her only through means that were likely to destabilise his position on the Continent. At the same time, Austria had been treated in a fashion so brutal that it could not but create a powerful war party in Vienna. Even friendship, indeed, was no protection: when Frederick William objected to the terms of Prussia's treaty with Napoleon, he was threatened with war and forced to accept conditions that were even worse than before; in the same way, Switzerland was menaced with military occupation for having allegedly failed to provide Napoleon with sufficient troops. Austerlitz, in short, had settled nothing, while showing the French emperor to the world in his true colours.

Time chart 4: 1806–7

1806

March	Revolt breaks out in Calabria.
August	Prussia enters the war.
October	Campaign of Jena; Russia attacks Turkey.
November	Continental Blockade inaugurated by the Decree of Berlin; French occupy Prussian Poland.

1807

February	Russians defeated at Eylau (Bagrationovsk).
March–April	British invade Egypt.
June–July	Russians defeated at Friedland (Pravdinsk) and make peace at Tilsit (Sovetsk).

4

The War of the Fourth Coalition

After Austerlitz, France could justly be regarded as the dominant European power. Austria had been humbled, Prussia cowed into becoming an ally, Naples transformed into a satellite state, and Russia forced effectively to withdraw from hostilities. Britain was still in action, but her only ally was a Sweden that was possessed of a negligible army, deeply divided and perpetually at odds with London over the question of subsidies. Once again, in short, peace seemed a real possibility, and yet it never came. Why, then, was this the case?

If the struggle continued, it was not the fault of Britain and Russia, both of which genuinely tried to make peace. Badly shaken, Alexander was no longer able to strike directly at Napoleon except in the Adriatic, where the Russians were impeding the annexation of Dalmatia. Deeply mistrustful of British attempts to get him to go to war with Prussia (which he rightly saw as merely a scheme to recover Hanover), and increasingly concerned that Napoleon might entangle him with Austria and the Ottoman Empire and send help to Persia, which had been at war with Russia since 1804, the tsar opened peace negotiations. Meanwhile, the belligerent Pitt government having been replaced in the wake of its leader's recent death by a new ministry dominated by proponents of a compromise peace, emissaries were soon on the way from London as well.

Once again, however, Napoleon rendered peace impossible, since he would make none of the concessions necessary to secure a settlement, nor still less moderate his treatment of vassal state or defeated enemy alike. By the summer, then, negotiations had lapsed, but, even so, neither Britain nor Russia prosecuted the war in an effective fashion. On the contrary, the British blockaded Prussia, wasted troops in 'pinprick' operations on the Italian coast and allowed themselves to become embroiled in a futile series of operations whose object was the emancipation of Spain's colonies in South America, while for the time being Russia abandoned any thought of operations in central Europe and instead became more and more preoccupied with the situation in the Balkans. Thus, not only was there real concern that Napoleon was seeking an alliance with the Ottoman Empire, but the tsar was deeply influenced by the idea of the creation of Polish, Romanian, Serbian and Greek puppet states and in consequence dreaming of ejecting the Turks from such areas as Moldavia and Wallachia.

If the continental war was suddenly revived, it was in fact the work of Prussia. Thus, following his treaty with Napoleon, Frederick William had suddenly discovered the limits of the emperor's friendship. With Prussia's trade badly hit by the British blockade, in July 1806 Napoleon organised his new Confederation of the Rhine – initially a league of fourteen central and south German states whose central purpose was to supply the emperor with a large contingent of auxiliaries – without any reference to Prussia. To add insult to injury, the emperor suggested that Frederick William should form a confederation of his own in northern Germany, while at the same time inciting the states concerned to reject the whole idea. Still worse, it then transpired that the abortive negotiations with the British had seen Napoleon offer to return Hanover to Britain, a most unwilling Frederick William finally being forced into a declaration of war.

The campaign that followed was dramatic indeed. Denied support – the British would spare the Prussians neither men nor money, while the Russians had no troops ready to send to their aid – the Prussians mobilised 145,000 men in Thuringia. However, invading Saxony, Napoleon got round their eastern flank and threatened their communications with Berlin. Desperate to escape, the Prussians fled north-eastwards, only to collide with the *grande armée* in the vicinity of the River Saale, where on 14 October 1806 they were heavily defeated at the linked battles of Jena and Auerstädt. In view of the great debate that was precipitated in Prussia by these events after 1806, it is worth pointing out that the Prussians were not defeated by either lack of enthusiasm among their soldiery or old-fashioned tactics. What destroyed them was rather a combination of defective organisation, lack of co-ordination and poor command and control, in that their light infantry, artillery and cavalry were all marshalled in an inefficient fashion, their forces split into a number of separate columns, and their commander, the mediocre Duke of Brunswick, hampered by the presence of Frederick William IV and the resentment of many of his fellow generals.

However, if Jena and Auerstädt were by no means a disgrace, what followed was by any standards a catastrophe. Thus, no sooner had the guns fallen silent than the victorious French armies launched an invasion of Prussia that carried all before it. Broken into several fragments and reduced to a state of semi-starvation, most of what remained of the Prussian army was rounded up with hardly a fight, while many fortresses capitulated at the first summons. Berlin fell without resistance on 24 October, while everywhere the populace remained quiet. Prussia was not yet out of the war – Frederick William had escaped to the east with a few troops – while a little honour was redeemed by gallant attempts at resistance at Halle and Lübeck, but Napoleon's triumph was still overwhelming.

Ensconced in Berlin, Napoleon could not have felt greater confidence in his abilities as a conqueror, while he was now ready to avenge himself on Britain. Hence the famous 'Decree of Berlin' of 21 November 1806. Supreme at sea, Britain was to be defeated by the power of the land. Thus, throughout the territories ruled by or allied to France, all commerce with Britain was to be ended and all British ships and their cargoes seized. The result, it was hoped, was that Britain would sooner or later be forced to surrender. With this scenario there was but one problem, in that the decree signalled nothing less than an aspiration to universal mastery. Often acceptable in the short term – the British had, after all, been interfering in the commercial freedoms of the Continent – in the long term, such was the disruption that was likely to result that sooner or later French soldiers would have to police the embargo. No state could hope for peace unless it followed the policy's stipulations, meanwhile, for its only hope of success was the closure of the whole of Europe to Britain's trade. At Berlin, in short, Napoleon committed himself to a course which had no other end than total victory.

What made matters still worse was the fact that the blockade contained within it the seeds of a grand design of the most exploitative sort. British exports and re-exports were to be excluded from the Continent, certainly, but no attempt was ever made to turn this situation to the benefit of the whole of Europe. On the contrary, the blockade was from the start an integral part of an economic policy designed to harness the rest of Europe to France's needs. In particular, French industry was to be protected and the rest of the Continent transformed – literally – into a captive market. In short, what the Decree of Berlin presaged was nothing less than a Europe cast as a vast 'uncommon market' – indeed, a colonial empire.

Before the full impact of the Continental Blockade could be revealed, however, Napoleon still had a war to win. Protected by the onset of winter, Frederick William was still holding out in East Prussia amidst desperate efforts to remedy the defects of what was left of the Prussian army; in Stralsund 9,000 Swedish troops were ready to defend themselves against French attack; and large numbers of Russians were marching west to join the Prussians, Alexander I having decided that he could not simply abandon them to their fate. As Austria might conceivably seize the opportunity to attack the emperor in the rear, speed was of the essence. By 28 November the advanced guard of the *grande armée* had therefore reached Warsaw, where they were soon joined by Napoleon himself.

In marching east, Napoleon also had other motives. Many of the Polish gentry were desperate to restore Poland's independence, while they also regarded France as a potential saviour. As he had hoped, indeed, no sooner had Napoleon entered Warsaw than a junta of notables was established to administer the territories occupied by the French. No specific promises were given about the future for fear of hardening the resolve of Prussia and Russia or inducing the Austrians to enter the war, but broad hints were dropped that a substantial military effort might well produce the desired result. If all this was expected to produce wholesale insurrection, however, Napoleon was disappointed. Considerable elements even of the aristocracy remained hostile, while the populace were simply indifferent to the nationalist appeal. In the event, sufficient men were found to raise an army of 40,000, but this success was in large part the fruit of poverty and despair. The whole affair has been much mythologised, the fact being that the Polish 'war of liberation' of 1807 was no more a national war than its German counterpart of 1813.

Elsewhere, meanwhile, Napoleon had met with better fortune. Throughout 1806 the emperor had been looking to Turkey as a potential ally against Russia. With relations between Constantinople and St Petersburg strained not just by a long history of conflict, but by the increasingly successful Serbian revolt and differences over Moldavia and Wallachia, clever diplomacy had soon shattered the

Russo-Turkish alliance of 1799. With the Russians provoked into invading the Danubian principalities, Constantinople obliged by declaring war first on Russia and then Britain. As the Turkish forces were overstretched by the Serbian revolt and a variety of other problems, they were unable to make much impression on the Russians. On the contrary, the latter had by the close of the year occupied almost the whole of Moldavia and Wallachia even if substantial Russian forces were for years to be tied down in a bloody conflict.

To return to Poland, Napoleon did not follow up the occupation of Warsaw as rapidly as might have been expected, much time being needed to rest and re-equip the *grande armée* and gather the magazines needed for a winter campaign in an area of Europe that was particularly poor. Despite the fact that the Russian army was now concentrated only fifty miles to the north of Warsaw, it was therefore not until 22 December that the French moved forward again. However, the advance was slowed by atrocious weather, while the Russians bought time with a number of fierce delaying actions and in the end got clean away, a frustrated emperor being left with no option but to order his exhausted and hungry troops to break off the pursuit. However, the respite proved short-lived, the threat of a Russian counter-offensive eventually precipitating an advance deep into East Prussia. Initially, the Russians fell back without a fight, but on 7 February Napoleon caught up with them at Eylau (Bagrationovsk), the result being perhaps the most dreadful battle of the entire French Wars. Ensconced in a strong defensive position and aided by howling blizzards, the Russians fought the French to a standstill. Had they held on through the night, indeed, it is possible that they might have scored a notable defensive victory, but in the last resort their commander's nerve failed him and he therefore fell back on Königsberg (Kaliningrad).

Such was the blow which Napoleon suffered at Eylau that a vigorous offensive elsewhere might have brought real success. However, it was not to be. More and more troops having been sucked into the South American imbroglio, Britain limited herself to ineffectual operations against the Ottoman Empire in Egypt and the Dardanelles, while providing little in the way of arms, supplies or money. Some effort, it is true, was made to persuade Austria to stab Napoleon in the back, but even then subsidies were only offered in the event of Vienna actually entering the war, the result being that the substantial party in the Austrian court that was opposed to any resumption of hostilities was easily able to maintain the upper hand.

Battered and bleeding though he was, Napoleon was therefore allowed to recover the initiative. Within six weeks of Eylau, indeed, the *grande armée* was once again on the move. Stralsund had already been under siege since the end of January, and it was now joined by the Prussian strongholds of Danzig (Gdansk) and Kolberg (Kolobrszeg). More importantly, meanwhile, a Russian counter-offensive led to a decisive confrontation at the town of Friedland (Pravdinsk), the battle that followed on 14 June shattering the Fourth Coalition beyond repair. Caught with their backs to a river, hugely outnumbered and with their positions overlooked by higher ground and divided by a sizeable stream that ran down to the river just north of the town, the Russians were crushed, Alexander in consequence deciding that he should ask for an armistice.

If Friedland had been a shattering blow to Alexander, it was not the only reason why he decided to make peace. In brief, he suspected that the British had only established themselves in Egypt to counter Russian expansion in the Balkans and the Levant, he resented their failure to force the Dardanelles, and he could not but feel that the current British government set far more store on Britain's interests in the wider world than on the struggle in Europe. On 26 March, it is true that the more vigorous Portland administration had supplanted the so-called 'Talents', while the new Foreign Secretary, George Canning, had immediately promised both a substantial increase in subsidies and a British expeditionary force, but this was a question of 'too little, too late', while there was in any case no way that troops could be transported to the Baltic in the short term. Less important but just as irritating, meanwhile, were the actions of the Swedes, who had not only failed to provide Kolberg and Danzig with the naval support that might have been expected, but also seized £80,000 that had been *en route* to St Petersburg as part of the British subsidy.

If Alexander was thoroughly disillusioned with all and sundry by the summer of 1807, irritation was not the only motive for his conduct. Setting aside the fact that much of the Russian nobility were pressing for peace – an ominous development that could not but have brought to mind the fate of the murdered Paul I – Russia's foreign policy aims did not in themselves require a war with France. Thus, the establishment of a Russian sphere of influence in eastern Europe presupposed the partition of Poland and the Ottoman Empire, but did not stand in the way of French control of Belgium, the Rhineland, Germany or northern Italy, or even a French presence in the Balkans. Given that France and Russia had a common interest in combating Britain's pretensions on the high seas, it seemed that peace with France might even produce much profit.

The events that followed are well known. On 25 June Napoleon and Alexander met on a specially constructed raft that had been moored in the centre of the River Niemen (Neman) at Tilsit (Sovetsk). Friendly relations were soon established – Napoleon, in particular, appears to have made the greatest possible effort to charm the impressionable Alexander – while the awkward problem presented by the war in the Balkans was glossed over by the pretence that France's alliance with the Ottoman Empire had been the fruit of a personal accord between Napoleon and Sultan Selim III, the point being that the latter had been toppled in a palace coup in Constantinople on 27 May. Negotiations lasted until 9 July, but, so far as France and Russia were concerned, there was little difficulty in coming to an arrangement. Unlike most of Napoleon's victims, Russia was required to surrender neither money nor territory. Indeed, she actually obtained a sizeable slice of Prussian Poland, in return for which she granted Napoleon a free hand in Europe, recognised the Napoleonic settlement in Italy, Germany, the Low Countries and Poland, agreed to French occupation of the Ionian Isles and Cattaro (Kotor) and committed herself to joining the Continental Blockade, going to war with Britain, and forcing Sweden, Denmark and Austria to do the same. Concealed here was permission for a descent on Swedish Finland, while Russian hegemonism was also flattered by agreement that Alexander might dispatch a large army against Persia as a first step in a march on India. As for the Ottoman Empire, Napoleon would first press favourable peace terms upon Constantinople, and – assuming they were rejected – go to war against the Turks himself, in which event the goal would be to partition the whole of the Balkans between France and Russia.

On the surface at least, then, Russia did quite well out of Tilsit, Alexander coming away believing that Napoleon was both a friend and a partner. The same, however, could not be said for Prussia. Thus, the latter was forced to pay a heavy indemnity, reduce her army to 42,000 men, maintain a large French garrison, recognise the Confederation of the Rhine, which was now expanded to include the whole of Germany apart from Prussia and Austria, accede to the Continental Blockade, and accept the loss of half her territory. In this latter respect her western territories and Prussian Poland were seized to form the new states of Berg, Westphalia and the Grand Duchy of Warsaw (of which Berg was handed to Napoleon's brother-in-law

Joachim Murat, Westphalia to his brother Jerome, and the Grand Duchy of Warsaw to the King of Saxony; a small district – East Friesland – also went to Louis Bonaparte as King of Holland).

Tilsit, then, found the Napoleonic Empire at what proved to be its zenith. Napoleon himself was the unchallenged ruler of a much enlarged France; French potentates had been placed on the thrones of Holland, Berg, Westphalia, Naples and the Kingdom of Italy; Germany and Switzerland were entirely under French control, and Spain was a humble ally. Britain, meanwhile, could still count on the support of Sweden, but her supremacy at sea had availed her very little: not only had she failed to make any impact at all in the campaigns of October 1806 to June 1807, but her various expeditionary forces had come to a bad end. Thus, twice defeated at Rosetta (Rashid), the British force that had been sent to Egypt was soon blockaded in Alexandria (al-Iskandariya), while its South American counterpart was forced to capitulate on 5 July after a bungled attack on Buenos Aires. As for her vigorous response to the Continental Blockade, the Orders-in-Council in which this resulted bade fair to plunge Britain into fresh complications on account of the tight controls they imposed on neutral shipping. With Napoleon in control of much of the European coastline, the future was distinctly uncertain.

What would have occurred next is impossible to say, but such was Britain's predicament that it is entirely possible that she could once again have been forced to come to terms. Fortunately for the new administration of the Duke of Portland, however, their opponent was not a rational European statesman but Napoleon. If he had allowed Russia to believe that she was a French partner rather than a French vassal, the emperor might have won the war; but, once again, he could not let matters be. In short, if England stood all but alone, she would not do so for very long.

Time chart 5: 1807–11

1807

July	Napoleon establishes Grand Duchy of Warsaw.
August	French occupy Ionian islands.
August–September	British invade Denmark and seize Danish navy.
September	British evacuate Egypt.
October	French forces enter Spain and invade Portugal.

1808

February	France occupies Rome; Russia invades Finland.
March	France annexes Tuscany, Parma and Piacenza; Charles IV of Spain deposed in riots at Aranjuez.
May	Spanish Bourbons overthrown in favour of Joseph Bonaparte; revolt erupts in Spain.
June	National uprising breaks out in Portugal.
July	French suffer severe reversals in Spain.
August	British liberate Portugal.
November–December	Napoleon restores French position in Spain.

1809

March	French re-invade Portugal; Gustav IV of Sweden overthrown by a military coup.
April	Revolt breaks out in the Tyrol; Austria re-enters war.
May	French again expelled from Portugal.
July	Austrians sign armistice of Znaim (Znojmo) after being defeated at Wagram.
September	Sweden makes peace with Russia.
October	Tyrolean revolt collapses.

1810

January	French conquer Andalucía.
April	Spanish–American revolution begins in Venezuela.
July	France annexes Holland; French re-invade Portugal.
December	France annexes Oldenburg, Hanseatic towns, and parts of Hanover and Berg.

1811

January–March	French conquer Extremadura, but are driven from Portugal; Calabrian revolt collapses.
June–December	French conquer southern Catalonia and the Levante.

5

The War of the Fifth Coalition

At no point in the French Wars did matters look quite so bleak for Britain as they did in the summer of 1807. To military humiliation in Egypt and South America was added catastrophe in Europe, for Napoleon was now in a position to subject Britain to a policy of strangulation, while constructing new fleets of such a size that it seemed that even the Royal Navy might be driven from the seas. Nor was it likely that Britain would get help from any of the great powers: setting aside the fact that they had each taken a terrible battering, London's enforced exploitation of its naval and commercial superiority was alienating all and sundry.

Unlike in 1806, however, there was no talk of peace: the Portland administration was dominated by two men – Canning and Castlereagh – whose determination to oppose the French was unparalleled. Both Egypt and South America were evacuated, it is true, but the troops that had been gathered for the Baltic were not held back on account of Friedland, while the news of Tilsit was simply shrugged off. Far from crumpling up, indeed, the Portland administration launched a rapid pre-emptive strike. Thus, alarm had been growing at the possibility that neutral Denmark's fleet would be seized by the French. In consequence, a substantial British expedition was sent to Copenhagen, while the Danes were offered the choice of a defensive alliance or war. The Danes chose the latter, and Copenhagen was invested and bombarded into surrender, the Danish fleet then being taken to England. However, success came at a heavy cost. Civilian casualties had run into thousands, while the speed with which the British had rushed to secure their interests did not sit well with the dilatory manner in which they had responded to Austrian or Prussian pleas for assistance. Not surprisingly, meanwhile, Denmark declared war, while Sweden, too, was furious, many of the British troops sent to the Baltic having originally been intended for the defence of Stralsund, which had been under French attack since January and eventually fell on 10 August.

Pre-empting one danger, in short, had simply created other difficulties. Meanwhile, the Continental Blockade was beginning to bite. At this stage Britain had still not acquired the alternative markets that were to be the central factor in her salvation, while the smuggling that was now the only means by which British cargoes could reach most of the Continent required a degree of risk that many merchants were as yet unwilling to contemplate. With many important raw materials increasingly scarce, by late 1807 Britain was experiencing a deep recession. Wool and cotton were badly hit, and many textile manufacturers became involved in a growing peace movement. Meanwhile, social unrest was clearly on the increase, the spring of 1808 witnessing a rash of major strikes.

With the blockade tightened still further by the so-called 'Decrees of Milan', Britain could have been in real trouble. Patience might therefore have brought Napoleon a great deal, but patience was not something that the emperor possessed, while he was in any case convinced that dramatic action was essential to his rule. In Italy, then, the short-lived Kingdom of Etruria (i.e. Tuscany) was annexed by France. More dramatically still, Spain was persuaded to join with France in the invasion of neutral Portugal, which remained an outpost of British trade. By the end of November, indeed, Lisbon had been occupied, by which time Napoleon had signed a secret treaty with Spain which stipulated that Portugal was to be divided into three separate parts of which one was to be awarded to the Spanish royal favourite, Manuel de Godoy; one to the Queen of Etruria as the daughter of Charles IV of Spain; and one left under French occupation. Needless to say, it had also been intended that the ruling Bragança dynasty should be deposed and the Portuguese fleet commandeered for imperial service, but at the last moment royal family and ships alike fled to the safety of the Atlantic Ocean across which they eventually made their way to Brazil.

The occupation of Portugal was followed by intervention in Spain, the latter not only proving distinctly unsatisfactory as an ally – as witnessed Trafalgar, where the Spanish fleet had been seen to be in dire straits in terms of its combat capacity – but showing signs of wanting to break free of the French embrace. To understand the events that followed, it is necessary to note how weak Spain's position was. Long years of warfare had produced much economic disruption, the effects of which had been heightened by a series of natural disasters. Meanwhile, matters were not helped by the fact that the monarchy was possessed of the highly reformist disposition typical of enlightened absolutism. Though this stirred up discontent in a variety of contexts, perhaps its most serious effect came in the countryside: eager to break the power of the clergy, to raise money for the war effort and to encourage agricultural innovation, from 1798 onwards the regime had been expropriating the estates of the Church and selling them on the open market. By 1808, indeed, one-sixth of the land involved had been sold, the general effect being to force up the rents paid by the Church's erstwhile tenants.

Although these policies caused much social unrest, in many respects this was the least of the regime's problems. Resentment had been growing for some time at the monarchy's assault on the privileged corporations, of which the most notable were the Church and the nobility. From 1792 this anger had been crystallised in the resentment aroused by Manuel de Godoy. A scion of the petty nobility who had risen to favour in the court, Godoy had in that year been made chief minister by Charles IV, who was determined to place power in the hands of a man who was entirely his creature. As such, Godoy had pursued reform with vigour, with the result that he had inevitably incurred much anger. Very soon, indeed, a party that opposed his pre-eminence had coalesced around the figure of the heir to the throne, Prince Ferdinand, who allowed himself to be persuaded, first, that Godoy was seeking to become the next king of Spain, and second, that the best way to secure his own future was to win Napoleon's friendship.

By the autumn of 1807 matters had reached boiling point. Thus, on 27 October a search of Ferdinand's apartments uncovered papers that hinted at a plot to overthrow Charles IV and Godoy alike, Ferdinand being placed under arrest and his chief collaborators imprisoned. Though the prince was soon released, the result was French inter-vention. Unwilling to see Spain slide into anarchy, Napoleon resolved on a military takeover. Helped by a general belief that the emperor was aiming only at the overthrow of Godoy and enthronement of Ferdinand, in February 1808 Napoleon's troops occupied the main

Spanish border fortresses. Realising that his strategy – essentially a military revival under cover of an alliance with France – was in ruins, Godoy tried to organise resistance and get the royal family to South America, but his every effort was interpreted as an attempt to escape retribution. Meanwhile, the conspirators who surrounded Ferdinand realised that they had to take immediate action to save the prince, whom they regarded as a mere puppet. Acting through sympathetic contacts in the royal guard, they therefore organised a military coup at the royal residence of Aranjuez, forced Charles IV to abdicate, arrested Godoy, and proclaimed Ferdinand king of Spain.

Desperate efforts now followed to conciliate Napoleon, but the emperor was unresponsive. With his forces now in Madrid, the entire royal family was persuaded to travel to Bayonne for a conference at which Charles and Ferdinand were browbeaten into surrendering the Spanish throne in favour of Joseph Bonaparte. If he had believed that the Bourbons could be removed quietly, however, Napoleon was sorely mistaken. On the contrary, sporadic disturbances, of which the most notable was a serious rising in Madrid, had become a full-scale national uprising by the end of May. Of all the events of the French Wars, there is probably none that has been more misunderstood. Generally portrayed as the product of outraged patriotism, the rising was actually a distinctly murky affair that reflected many of the different tensions besetting the body politic. Thus, the various provincial risings – for there was no concerted uprising as such – were engineered by a variety of dissident groups. The insurrection's leaders included disgruntled office-seekers, radicals eager to make a political revolution, prominent civilians resentful of the privileges of the military estate, discontented subaltern officers eager for promotion, conservative clerics horrified by Bourbon anti-clericalism, and members of the aristocracy opposed to the creeping advance of royal authority. As for the crowd, meanwhile, its motivation was as much material as it was ideological. It is true there was intense loyalty to Ferdinand VII, but this stemmed not so much from who he was as from what he represented, Godoy's enemies having deliberately portrayed Ferdinand as a species of Prince Charming who would solve all Spain's problems, while the response it called forth was not a rush to the colours, but rather an attack on the propertied classes.

Before continuing further in our discussion of Spain and Portugal (where the Spanish example was quickly followed), it is necessary to examine the north of Europe. In brief, Sweden was now discovering the implications of Tilsit. Thus, on 21 February 1808 Sweden was attacked by Russia whose troops quickly occupied much of Finland (then a Swedish possession). As time went on, resistance stiffened, but even so, 7 May saw the capitulation of the major fortress of Sveaborg (Suomenlinna). Russia having soon been joined by Denmark, which quickly received the assistance of a considerable detachment of the *grande armée*, it appeared that the Swedish heartland was at risk of invasion, and a substantial British expeditionary force was in consequence dispatched to Gothenburg (Goteborg). However, the arrival of this force was followed within a few days by the news of the revolt in Spain, while relations between the British and Gustav IV proved turbulent in the extreme. Presented with a more convenient alternative, London therefore withdrew its land forces. Assisted by a British naval squadron, the Swedes fought on, but to all intents and purposes they had been written off.

To return to Iberia, matters were by no means going well for Napoleon. Largely composed of second-line troops, the French forces in Spain were widely scattered, and their initial attempts to suppress the insurrection suffered several set-backs. Still worse, a bungled action at Bailén on 19 July was followed by the surrender of some 20,000 men, whereupon the recently arrived Joseph Bonaparte panicked and withdrew all the men at his disposal to a position of safety north of the Ebro. With the French forces in Catalonia blockaded in Barcelona, by early August Spain was completely out of control. To make matters worse, meanwhile, 1 August had seen the disembarkation of a British expeditionary force in Portugal under the initial command of the future Duke of Wellington (then Sir Arthur Wellesley), the garrison being defeated at Vimeiro and left with no option but to capitulate.

With the French position in the Peninsula reduced to a mere toe-hold, the insurgents were now able to organise themselves politically. Her royal family having escaped to Brazil, in the case of Portugal all that was required was the formation of a council of regency. However, matters were very different in Spain. In brief, power initially lay in the hands of a number of hastily improvised provincial juntas and military dictatorships. Prompted by a variety of factors, in September 1808 these independent local governments established a federal authority known as the Junta Central, which sat first at Aranjuez and then at Seville. However, this was not an end to the matter, for not only were many of the provincial authorities unwilling to recognise the government they had created, but assorted aristocratic generals were anxious to establish a regency controlled by themselves as a firm bulwark against any further encroachment on the rights of the nobility.

With all this going on, the Spaniards were not unnaturally slow to assemble their armies on the Ebro. Meanwhile, however, the emperor had been pouring fresh troops into Spain. By the beginning of November, indeed, an overwhelming strike force was ready for action under Napoleon himself. Smashing through the Spanish centre, the French had within a month reoccupied Madrid, inflicted heavy defeats on the Spaniards at Tudela and Espinosa de los Monteros, and relieved Barcelona. Shortly afterwards, Galicia, too, was overrun, following a British attempt to cut Napoleon's communications that ended in the evacuation of their army from La Coruña. Zaragoza defied a siege until 19 February 1809, but otherwise almost the whole of northern Spain had been cleared of regular resistance.

Returning to France, Napoleon delegated to his commanders what seemed to him the simple task of ending resistance once and for all. No such result was attained, however. An invasion of northern Portugal got as far as Oporto before being thrown back by Wellington, but in Spain it was rather the Spaniards who assumed the offensive, the Junta Central being determined to win back the key cities of Madrid and Zaragoza. With much of the French zone of occupation bedevilled by growing popular resistance, the French drew back a little, but even with the aid of the British – in July 1809 Wellington entered Spain and took part in a drive on Madrid – the attacks proved unsuccessful. On the contrary, ill-trained, ill-supplied and lacking in adequate cavalry and artillery, the Spaniards were repeatedly defeated. Spanish losses were enormous, but they could not be made up, and all the more so as the populace showed little enthusiasm for conscription. Wellington's foray across the frontier having left the British in no doubt as to the inadvisability of further adventures in Spain, the Spanish armies were all but helpless by the end of 1809.

If Spain had not been conquered by the end of 1809, it was largely the result of events elsewhere. Although his domains had by no means been untroubled in the two years that followed Tilsit – in Calabria, in particular, peasant insurgents had been waging a fierce guerrilla struggle – the emperor had thus far been able to concentrate the whole of his endeavours upon the Peninsula. In 1809, however, the situation underwent a dramatic change. Heavily defeated in 1805 and subjected to a diet of constant humiliation thereafter, Austria had maintained a low profile until 1808. Under the leadership of the Archduke Charles, the army was strengthened by a variety of military reforms, but Charles himself believed that Vienna should cut its losses in Germany and Italy, abandon all notion of fighting Napoleon, and seek compensation in the Balkans. As for the Emperor Francis – since 6 August 1806 Francis I of Austria rather than Francis II of the Holy Roman Empire – he remained as cautious as ever, all the more so as Russia was now a potential enemy. For a brief time, indeed, an alliance was sought with Napoleon, but it soon emerged that the emperor was simply not interested in such a deal. Still worse, indeed, his overthrow of the Spanish Bourbons provoked fears that he might treat the Habsburgs in the same fashion. Though still hopeful that war might be avoided, Vienna therefore accelerated military reform and began to stir up German nationalism. If the object was to secure better treatment from Napoleon, however, the effort was a futile one. Having secured promises of Russian co-operation at a further meeting with Alexander at Erfurt in September 1808, the emperor kept up the pressure, and on 23 December the increasingly desperate Francis resolved on war.

Needless to say, the Austrians endeavoured to secure help from Russia, Prussia and Britain alike, but the first was uninterested in a breach with Napoleon and bound by treaty to go to war against them; the second cowed and in large part under military occupation; and the third unwilling to support Austria with either men or money until she actually went to war. Aside from a revolt in the Tyrol – where the local inhabitants had become increasingly resentful of Bavarian rule – when the Austrian armies went into action on 9 April 1809, they did so unsupported (the only bright spot was that, unwilling to see Austria neutralised altogether, the Russians secretly promised her that they would enter the war in name alone). Initially, however, Austrian success was considerable. Napoleon having been caught napping, the Archduke Charles overran much of eastern Bavaria, while other armies occupied much of the Grand Duchy of Warsaw, the Kingdom of Italy and the Tyrol, where the local insurgents had soon eliminated the inadequate Bavarian garrison.

Austria's success proved short-lived, however. Despite efforts to whip up revolt, the rest of Germany remained quiet, with the result that Napoleon was able to drive Charles back and occupy Vienna. Threatened with encirclement, the Austrian forces in the Tyrol and northern Italy promptly retreated, while the Poles counter-attacked and invaded Galicia. On 21–22 May an attempt by Napoleon to resume the offensive was admittedly repulsed by Charles at Aspern-Essling with heavy losses, but in Italy the Austrians were beaten at the River Piave and forced to retreat to Hungary where they were defeated for a second time at Raab (Gyor). Meanwhile a Russian army occupied Cracow. The *coup de grâce*, however, came at the battle of Wagram. Fought just outside Vienna on 5–6 July, this was a titanic struggle that saw Napoleon secure a narrow victory. For the outnumbered Austrians it was a respectable performance, but Charles knew that his forces would not be able to endure another battle and therefore asked for an armistice.

The Austrian collapse was not quite the end of the story, but Napoleon's position was now unassailable. By the time of Wagram, Sweden was effectively out of the war: following a series of reverses, on 13 March Gustav IV had been overthrown by an aristocratic faction determined to put an end to enlightened absolutism and restore Sweden's traditional alliance with France. As for the British, meanwhile, 1809 was marked by an episode that was virtually epic in its futility. Desirous not so much of aiding Austria as of striking a further blow against French naval power, the Portland administration had decided to launch an assault on Antwerp. After much delay a large army was duly assembled for this purpose, and by 30 July the first British troops were going ashore. Flushing (Vlissingen) was captured, but the British advance was so slow that the defenders had time to reinforce Antwerp to such an extent that an attack proved impracticable. It is true that Walcheren Island remained in British hands, but its climate provoked an epidemic of malaria so terrible that it eventually had to be abandoned. Only in Germany – where, despite Wagram, a flying-column known as the Brunswick Black Corps had chosen to fight on – Tyrol and Calabria did active hostilities continue, but here too the French and their allies had the upper hand: the Brunswickers were forced to set sail for Britain, the Tyroleans were gradually hunted down and the Calabrian *banditti* subjected to ever greater pressure. On the debit side, the British had succeeded in occupying most of the Ionian islands, but on the whole French arms ruled supreme.

All that remains to be said of the campaigns of 1809 is the territorial adjustments to which they gave rise. Needless to say, the chief casualty was Austria. Carinthia, Carniola and part of Croatia were added to the territories lost in Istria and Dalmatia in 1805, and the city-state of Ragusa (Dubrovnik), which had been occupied by the French in 1807, to form the French-ruled Illyrian provinces; the portion of central Poland seized by Austria in 1795 was divided between Russia and the Grand Duchy of Warsaw; and Salzburg and some other border districts ceded to Bavaria. Meanwhile, Austria had to pay an indemnity of 85 million francs, reduce her army to 150,000 men, and join the Continental Blockade. Further resistance being impossible, salvation was now sought in a *détente* with France whose chief symbol was the marriage of the Archduchess Marie Louise to Napoleon, who had divorced Empress Josephine on account of her failure to produce an heir.

If these changes greatly extended French influence in the Balkans, they were not the only ones that had occurred in the course of 1808 and 1809. Thus, in Italy a variety of factors had led first to the occupation and then the annexation of Rome, while other casualties included Parma, Piacenza, Guastalla and Tuscany (the short-lived Kingdom of Etruria). Meanwhile, in Germany the newly created Grand Duchy of Berg had also lost all pretence of independence: its ruler, Napoleon's brother-in-law Joachim Murat, having been transferred to Naples following the departure of Joseph Bonaparte for Spain, the duchy had been placed under a French commissioner. Already, then, the blockade was exercising its malign influence, while Napoleon gave further proof of his refusal to tolerate the slightest opposition by having the pope arrested and deported to France.

With order restored in central Europe, Napoleon was once again free to concentrate on Iberia. Although he did not go there himself, the emperor therefore dispatched large reinforcements and ordered his commanders to regain the initiative. Thus, while one French strike force threatened the Patriot heartland of Andalucía, another massed against Portugal. Faced with the need to capture various Spanish fortresses that blocked its path, the latter did not cross the frontier until the summer, but in the south matters were very different. Reduced to a skeleton by the defeats of the previous year, the Spanish armies that protected Andalucía were simply swept aside, and by the end of January 1810 the French had therefore taken Seville and advanced to the Straits of Gibraltar. In the whole of Andalucía, indeed, the only stronghold left to the Spaniards was the island city of Cádiz, the latter now becoming host, first, to a new council of regency that was formed to replace the ill-fated provisional government of the period 1808 to 1810, and second, to the famous assembly known as the *cortes*.

Dominated by a group of radicals, the new assembly went on to give Spain a liberal constitution, abolish all forms of privilege and strip the

Church of its property. What the *cortes* could not do, however, was to influence the military situation. Deprived of a considerable proportion of their domestic income, the Spaniards simultaneously found themselves stripped of the copious financial assistance that had hitherto been arriving from their American empire, for in 1810 a variety of factors led to revolts in the areas that later became México, Venezuela, Colombia, Ecuador, Chile, Argentina, Paraguay and Uruguay. British aid remained plentiful, but even so the Spanish armies were unable to do much more than cling to the dwindling area of territory that remained free of French control. This was all the more the case as the British could not have undertaken any operations in Spain even had they wanted to: supported though he was by a reformed Portuguese army, in August 1810 Wellington was confronted by a massive French invasion force that drove straight for Lisbon and forced him to withdraw behind an impregnable series of fortifications which he had constructed just outside the capital. The countryside having been devastated in their path, it was expected that the French would have to retreat almost immediately, but in fact it was not until March 1811 that they began to fall back. Meanwhile, Wellington was unable to do more than bundle them over the frontier, and as the French were able to concentrate such forces against his repeated forays into Spain he was invariably left with no option but to retreat to Portugal.

With Wellington out of the way, the French were able to concentrate on crushing the Spaniards. Thus, Badajoz, Tortosa and Tarragona fell in 1811, and Valencia in January 1812, these reverses being accompanied by a litany of lost battles. All but incalculable, the Spanish losses could not be replaced, as all that was now left to the Patriot cause was part of Catalonia and the Levante, Cádiz and Galicia. As for America, it had simply become a burden, many troops having to be sent to the colonies. In effect, the Patriot cause was paralysed.

In view of the fame of the guerrillas who plagued the French in Spain, such a judgement might seem somewhat surprising; yet all was not as it seemed. While the French and their collaborators certainly experienced immense problems in Spain and Portugal alike, the popular resistance they faced varied enormously in its nature and impact. At the heart of the problem was the link that existed between guerrilla warfare and social protest, since many of the so-called guerrillas were little more than gangs of marauders driven from their homes by poverty and despair who preyed on all and sundry. Meanwhile, even when this was not the case – by 1810 many of the original bands had started to acquire a semi-regular status that allowed for greater control – the fact was that popular resistance did nothing to check the advance of the French armies. Indeed, but for the fact that the French were forced to employ large forces to contain Wellington and destroy the remnants of Spain's conventional armies, there seems no reason to suppose that the guerrillas would not ultimately have suffered the same fate as their Calabrian counterparts, the latter finally being suppressed in 1810.

A year after Wagram, then, the prospects for resistance to Napoleon seemed grim indeed. Austria and Sweden had effectively changed sides; Prussia was helpless; and Russia still a French ally. Meanwhile, if the Peninsular War continued to rage unabated, the Spaniards, at least, were in serious trouble. There was only one reason to take heart. Thus, by 1810 the implications of the Continental Blockade were starting to become all too apparent. Whereas the alliance with Spain and Portugal and the development of a variety of clandestine links with Europe had allowed the British to escape from its worst consequences, matters had become extremely difficult within the Napoleonic imperium. Prior to the imposition of the continental system, large areas of central and eastern Europe had been heavily dependent on the export of raw materials and agricultural products to Britain. This trade, however, was now cut off, while France was both unable to import bulk goods easily and self-sufficient in many of the products involved, the result being that agricultural prices, and with them purchasing power, could only fall. Yet, at the same time, French imports were disproportionately expensive, given France's technical deficiencies and transport problems. As French production rose (as it naturally did), so a crisis of over-production came ever closer, this being finally sparked off by new developments in the imposition of the Blockade. By 1810 Napoleon saw that he could not close the coasts to British trade, and further, that French industry was being held back by the high price of colonial goods. Meanwhile, the commerce raiding in which the French had been engaged since 1803 was becoming subject to the law of diminishing returns, the British having captured most of France's foreign bases. In response, the emperor decided that the only solution was to authorise the import of colonial goods while restricting this trade to France alone, a severe clamp-down being imposed on the huge stocks of contraband that existed in many German, Dutch and Italian cities.

Even in France these actions proved counter-productive. Speculation in colonial imports having become rife, the result was general ruin, with French merchants undercut by the new imports, and foreign ones stripped of their stocks. Both inside and outside France, the consequence was a squeeze on credit that produced a period of severe depression. As if all this was not enough, the period 1809 to 1811 was marked by abnormally severe weather, the price of food and industrial crops soaring by as much as 100 per cent. All this was inflicted against a background of steadily increasing taxation – the Peninsular War had ensured that Napoleon's conflicts had ceased to pay for themselves – and growing demands for fresh manpower. Deprived of such staples as coffee, chocolate, tobacco and sugar, and much bombarded by exhortations that they should emulate Spain and Portugal, the peoples of Europe might therefore have been expected to burst forth in revolt, but in fact all remained quiet. Yet for all that, the Napoleonic Empire remained inherently unstable: driven by the dictates of the Continental Blockade and his own character alike, by 1811 the emperor was heading for a fresh conflict that was to shake his dominions to their very core.

Time chart 6: 1812–14

1812

January–April	British launch counter-offensive in Spain.
April–May	Russia signs treaty of alliance with Sweden and makes peace with Turkey.
June	Napoleon invades Russia; war breaks out between Britain and the United States.
July–August	British liberate Madrid and force evacuation of Andalucía.
September	Napoleon enters Moscow.
October–December	French abandon Moscow and evacuate Russia; British evacuate northern and central Spain and retreat to Portugal.

1813

January–February	French evacuate East Prussia and Grand Duchy of Warsaw.
March	French evacuate all of Germany east of the Elbe; Prussia enters war against France.
May–June	French victories at Lützen and Bautzen secure armistice of Pläswitz.

June–August	Peace negotiations fail; Austria joins Russia and Prussia; French are driven from all of Spain except Catalonia.
August–October	Austrians invade Illyrian provinces and Kingdom of Italy; fierce fighting in Germany culminates in French defeat at Leipzig.
October–November	German states join Allies; British invade France; French evacuate Holland; Napoleon rejects Frankfurt proposals; Brunswick, Hanover and Hesse-Cassel restored as independent states.
December	Swedes invade Denmark; Serbian revolt collapses.

1814

January	Russians, Prussians and Austrians invade France; Naples joins Allies; Denmark surrenders to Sweden.
March	Allies agree Treaty of Chaumont; Ferdinand VII returns to Spain.
April	Napoleon abdicates at Fontainebleau.
May	Louis XVIII enters Paris; absolutism restored in Spain; Norway declares her independence; peace officially restored by first Treaty of Paris.
July–August	Swedes reconquer Norway.
September	Congress of Vienna begins.
December	United States and Britain sign Treaty of Ghent.

6

The War of the Sixth Coalition

As several observers of the period 1792 to 1815 have remarked, the French were better coalition-builders than their opponents. Impressive alliances had risen to challenge the French, but they had invariably been extremely fragile. While each coalition came and went, Paris was gradually cementing its control over an ever-lengthening list of allies and satellites. By contrast, Britain's record looks poor in the extreme: the only friends she had left by 1812 were Sicily, Spain and Portugal. As so often before, however, her greatest ally was Napoleon. Incapable of co-existing with any power on the basis of equality and apparently desirous of war for its own sake, by 1812 Napoleon had transformed Russia from friend into enemy, thereby precipitating the emergence of a coalition of such size and coherence that even he was unable to prevail against it.

Yet Napoleon's downfall was a long and painful process. Indeed, its roots may be traced at least as far back as 1808. Charmed by Napoleon as he was, Alexander had been perfectly sincere at Tilsit, believing that Russia had fared remarkably well, and that a deal with France was beneficial to Russia's interests and the only way to ensure peace in Europe. Meanwhile, already mistrustful of the British, he was infuriated by the attack on Copenhagen. Determined to make the alliance work, the tsar appointed the anti-British expansionist Count Nicholas Rumyantsev as foreign minister, his sincerity being further underlined by the fact that, such was the likely impact of the Continental Blockade on the Russian nobility, he was risking the same fate as his assassinated father. Napoleon had a sincere friend in Alexander, but within a year the tsar had come to the conclusion that another war was inevitable. In the first place, Tilsit brought few benefits. As expected, Russian trade with Britain collapsed. However, France could not make up the deficit, since transporting bulky products by land across Europe was not feasible (not that Napoleon did much to help: by 1810 even Rumyantsev was complaining of his tariff policy). Meanwhile, Alexander found that, whereas he had expected generous French assistance in the Balkans, the French ruler would only sanction the annexation of the Danubian provinces at the cost of detaching Silesia from Prussia, while making the general partition of Turkey's European territories desired by Alexander contingent on a Franco-Russian march on India.

If the French alliance was proving unsatisfactory, in other respects matters were becoming distinctly alarming. Thus fears grew that Napoleon was planning to add Russia's Polish territories to the Grand Duchy of Warsaw. Meanwhile, in the last resort both Prussia and Austria were essential to Alexander as a means of maintaining the balance of power, but both seemed to be in danger of further territorial losses. Finally, further afield, Napoleon was proceeding with the same lack of moderation that had so dismayed Alexander before 1805, the year that followed Tilsit witnessing the occupation of Spain, Portugal and what was left of the Papal States, the overthrow of the Spanish Bourbons, and the annexation of Tuscany.

In view of all this activity, Napoleon's Russian policy could not but appear in a most sinister light. While maintaining a show of friendship, Alexander therefore became far more obdurate, his resolution being hardened by the diplomatic developments that followed the war of 1809. Needing Russia's support against Britain, Napoleon now at last tried a policy of conciliation, handing Russia the Austrian border district of Tarnopol, reining in Polish ambitions, and opening negotiations for a marriage with the tsar's younger sister. Yet the emperor would not go so far as completely to rule out a restoration of the Kingdom of Poland, and outraged Alexander by switching his attentions to the rival bride offered by Austria, matters being made still worse by the emperor's decision to annex not only Holland, the Hanseatic states and a considerable part of Westphalia, but also the Duchy of Oldenburg, whose ruler happened to be Alexander's brother-in-law. Bavaria, meanwhile, was punished for its failures in the Tyrol by the transfer of its southernmost territories to the Kingdom of Italy, while France swallowed up the hitherto independent Swiss puppet-state known as the Republic of the Valais. By now the breach between the two rulers was virtually open, Alexander's response being to impose an anti-French tariff and to hint at the incorporation of the Grand Duchy of Warsaw into a Russian-dominated greater Poland. So angry was the tsar, indeed, that he seriously considered taking the offensive, only to back off for want of support. Nevertheless, preparations for war were soon underway: while the army was greatly expanded, a *rapprochement* was secured with Sweden and Turkey alike. As for Napoleon, he soon resolved that Alexander must be overborne, the winter of 1811 to 1812 therefore seeing the concentration of the largest army Europe had ever seen on the Russian frontier. Alexander refused to demobilise, and on 23 June 1812 Napoleon finally marched across the frontier.

Though Alexander may have flirted with the idea of taking the offensive, this was at best a momentary aberration. While making ready to defend himself, the tsar in fact tried hard to placate Napoleon and continued to enforce the Continental Blockade. Why, then, did Napoleon invade? Clearly not to enforce the Continental Blockade, for that was already being done. Did the emperor therefore believe his own claims that Russia was bent on attack? Perhaps so, but all the evidence suggests that underlying the invasion were other factors. First, Russia had to be restored to the fold of the emperor's continental system, Alexander's anti-French tariff having broken with the fundamental principle that required every part of Europe to be a captive market, and every ruler to be subservient to Napoleon himself. Second, Napoleon appears to have continued to harbour hopes of a march on India. Third, denied victory in Spain, the emperor may have increasingly felt a need to score another dramatic victory and even to conquer private fears relating to the onset of a combination of middle age, obesity and chronic ill-health.

Whatever its origins, there followed a conflict whose scope dwarfed anything thus far witnessed in the French Wars. Setting aside the largely Prussian and Austrian forces he had deployed to cover his flanks (the fruit of military alliances that those powers had just made with France), Napoleon had at least 375,000 men concentrated on the 75-mile front between Kovno (Kaunas) and Grodno, and another 80,000 in reserve. Facing these forces were no more than 175,000 Russians (though the substantial forces of regular troops that had been released by the recent agreements with Sweden and Turkey were slowly making their way towards White Russia, while large numbers of fresh conscripts were in the process of being called up).

Matters were not improved by the fact that the defenders were split into two separate armies whose commanders hated one another.

Yet the rapid victory Napoleon expected was not obtained. The emperor himself was in poor health, while bad roads, inadequate reconnaissance, commanders who were out of their depth and sheer size ensured that the *grande armée* moved with none of its customary speed. Evading three separate envelopments, the Russians therefore succeeded in concentrating their forces at Smolensk, leaving the invaders to lumber along in their wake. As Napoleon advanced, so his forces began to disintegrate. In the first place matters were not helped by the weather, periods of blazing heat being interspersed by torrential downpours. In the second the logistical situation collapsed, the troops outstripping their supply trains and discovering that the countryside in their path had been devastated by the retreating Russians. As a result, the 375,000 troops amassed by Napoleon had lost around 100,000 men by the time they reached Smolensk. Another 90,000 men having been detached to guard the road home, there remained but 182,000 front-line troops, losses of cavalry horses and draught animals having proportionately been even worse.

Nevertheless, all was not lost. Though the Russian armies had at last succeeded in coming together, they still numbered no more than 120,000 men. There was no victory, however, more bungling allowing the Russians to escape yet again, taking with them probably Napoleon's last chance of victory. As Alexander still refused to make peace, the emperor had no option but to march in pursuit, in the hope that he might yet force a decisive battle. Of this, however, there was now little hope. Given that the *grande armée* now began to encounter significant irregular resistance for the first time, the wastage consequent upon its advance increased still further. Meanwhile, 20,000 men had been lost at Smolensk and 16,000 more detached to act as its garrison. By the time the newly appointed Kutusov decided to give battle at Borodino some seventy miles west of Moscow, the odds against him had therefore been reduced still further, Napoleon's army now amounting to no more than 130,000 men.

Even now a crushing victory might still have brought success, and for a moment this again seemed to be in the emperor's grasp, Kutusov having not only deployed his army in such a position that it was in grave danger of being outflanked and trapped, but also arranged its command in a manner that can only be described as bizarre. Fortunately for him, however, on this occasion Napoleon's general-ship was even worse. In the first place, for no very good reason the emperor rejected the idea of envelopment, and instead settled upon a series of massive frontal assaults that led to heavy casualties and did no more than push the Russians back, while in the second, being tired and ill, he failed to throw the 18,000 men of the Imperial Guard who constituted his last reserve into the battle at the moment when it might have achieved a breakthrough.

Bloody draw though Borodino was, the war was lost. Though the French now entered Moscow without a fight, Napoleon could do no more. With Moscow set alight by Russian agents, partisan activity increasing, supplies desperately short, Kutusov's army a mere seventy-five miles to the south, substantial regular forces closing in on his thinly protected lines of communication, the discipline and morale of the *grande armée* at breaking point, and no more than 95,000 men available for action, the position was clearly desperate. Alexander again refused to make peace, and on 19 October Moscow was evacuated.

There followed the 'retreat from Moscow'. Vital time having been wasted by an abortive attempt to reach an alternative road to the west through countryside that had not yet been devastated, the *grande armée* was soon assailed by heavy snow and bitter cold as well as frequent attacks from not only the partisans but Kutusov's army as well. With the army encumbered by immense caravans of baggage and non-combatants, food, clothing and footwear in short supply, and exhausted by the endless retreat, formation after formation lost all cohesion as men died by the hundred or fell away to join the ever-growing crowd of stragglers. Barely escaping complete destruction when they were attacked from all sides at Berezina River, the survivors staggered on under the command of Marshal Ney (Napoleon himself fled by sleigh on 5 December), but they were forced to leave behind almost all the remaining guns and baggage and were eventually reduced to barely 20,000 men.

To conclude, the Russian campaign was a shattering blow, French losses having amounted to perhaps half a million men. Nor were the disasters of 1812 solely limited to the horrors that had occurred on the steppes. In Spain, for example, the Russian war had led to catastrophe. Thus, until 1811 a constant stream of replacements and reinforcements had allowed the French to contain the Anglo-Portuguese forces of the Duke of Wellington, while at the same time crushing regular Spanish resistance and beginning to hunt down the guerrillas. At the end of 1811, however, the French commanders were suddenly faced with demands that they should send back some of their troops to France. Not many men were involved, but the

French position was badly destabilised and all the more so as Napoleon also insisted that some of the troops containing Wellington should be switched to eastern Spain so as to ensure the success of the offensive that was currently in train against Valencia. Seizing his moment, Wellington immediately went over to the offensive, stormed the important border fortresses of Ciudad Rodrigo and Badajoz, and penetrated deep into Old Castile. Challenged by a substantial French army, he won a major victory at Salamanca on 22 July, and immediately moved on to occupy Madrid, whereupon the French were forced to evacuate the whole of Andalucía.

Having evacuated much of their conquests, the invaders were able to turn the tables on Wellington and force him to retreat to Portugal. For all that, the situation looked bleak. Badajoz, Ciudad Rodrigo and the whole of southern Spain remained in Allied hands, while in the Basque provinces and Navarre the guerrilla insurrection had acquired unprecedented force and effectiveness. While the Allied position was marred by a variety of disputes between the British and the Spaniards, it was therefore clear that the days of French success were over.

By the end of 1812, then, Napoleon's prestige had taken a terrible battering. Not surprisingly, this resulted in stirrings of a sort that a few months before would have been quite unthinkable. Even less surprisingly, meanwhile, the rot began in Prussia. Of all the states that Napoleon had overcome, Prussia was the one that had suffered worst. Stripped of much of her army, territory and population alike, and subjected not only to a heavy indemnity but to the Continental Blockade and semi-permanent French occupation, Prussia had had to pay a heavy price. Badly shaken, King Frederick William had therefore initiated a major programme of reform whose salient points included the emancipation of the serfs, the introduction of municipal self-government, and the improvement of the army by such means as the introduction of new tactics and the abolition of the noble monopoly in the officer corps. In the eyes of some of its progenitors – most notably, the Baron vom Stein – the aim of this programme was to create a situation in which the Prussian people would be encouraged to play an active role in the defence of the state, while in some cases they also wished to encourage the possibility of a great pan-German uprising. However, in the event other forces took hold: Stein was dismissed after incurring the wrath of Napoleon; the serfs were emancipated in such a way as to leave them worse off than before; and the king proved most unwilling to sanction the military measures needed to make popular resistance a reality.

To be frank, indeed, the Prussian reform movement had little or no impact on the international history of the Napoleonic period. That said, however, in the army in particular, many officers remained genuinely concerned at the extent to which Prussia had been humiliated. It is true that Frederick William had no intention of reneging on his alliance with Napoleon, but on 30 December the commander of the Prussian forces that had been sent into Russia to guard the communications of the *grande armée* signed a separate peace at Taurroggen (Taurage) and led his troops back into East Prussia, which had just been evacuated by the French. Having entered the service of Alexander I, meanwhile, Stein immediately rushed to Königsberg (Kaliningrad) as his commissioner and persuaded the local estates to decree the formation of a popular militia or *landwehr*. Needless to say, all this placed Frederick William in an impossible position. Terrified of Napoleon, suspicious of Russia, and deeply hostile to radical military reform, he at first sought to temporise. However, Napoleon's defeat having caused great excitement among the educated classes, the reformers were able to deluge the king with warnings of revolution, while it was also clear that failure to break with France might well be punished by the Russians. With many of his doubts assuaged by Russian guarantees that Prussia would be restored to a size equivalent to that of 1806 and the French now in full retreat to the south and west, Frederick William therefore finally entered the war while at the same time accepting such measures as the formation of volunteer units from among the well-to-do, the abolition of all exemptions from conscription, and the organisation of all those men not needed by the regular army into militias known as the *landwehr* and the *landsturm*.

To say that all this has given rise to a great deal of nonsense is an understatement. Within three months, the number of Prussians under arms had risen to some 270,000 men, while such enthusiasts for German nationalism as could be found – a very small number, be it said – had soon worked themselves up into a frenzy of patriotic enthusiasm. Meanwhile, in apparent emulation of the Spanish guerrillas, a variety of flying-columns were soon criss-crossing the countryside and striking deep into the French rear. That said, however, the fact was that outside Prussia few Germans were willing actually to take up arms against the French, while inside Prussia conscription was unpopular and desertion rife. As for the flying-columns, they were for the most part composed of Prussian regulars and Russian cossacks. This was truly a 'people's war without the people'.

Despite the fact that there was no popular uprising in Germany, the defection of Prussia (and, with her, Mecklenburg-Strelitz, which the French had evacuated at the same time) nevertheless gave rise to an entirely new situation. Thus Napoleon was opposed by not one but two coalitions. At one end of Europe stood Russia, Prussia, Sweden and Mecklenburg, and at the other Britain, Spain, Portugal and Sicily. In between the two, meanwhile, stood France, Holland, Denmark, the bulk of the Confederation of the Rhine, the Kingdom of Italy and Naples, Austria having hastily retreated into neutrality and the Grand Duchy of Warsaw succumbed to Russian occupation. Astonishingly enough, however, it was not until June that the two anti-Napoleonic leagues were brought together. In brief, the Russians both feared and mistrusted the British and were therefore inclined not only to refuse to allow themselves to be bound by London's views, but also to demand more than any British government could easily give in the way of subsidies and other support. As for the British, who were heavily committed in Iberia, they had become embroiled in a war with the United States over issues of trade. Happy enough to make peace with Sweden and Russia, London was therefore unwilling to send them help until it was clear that they were genuinely ready to strike a blow against Napoleon in Germany. In March 1813 an alliance was signed with Sweden, but such were the difficulties with Russia that it was three more months before the Sixth Coalition finally became a genuine entity.

Once agreement had been reached, however, British aid was extensive: by 1814 Prussia had received £2,088,682, Austria £1,639,523, Russia £3,366,334 and Sweden £2,334,992, while a small British expeditionary force was soon being readied for service in northern Germany. Given the problems that the Allies were to face in defeating Napoleon, this aid was vital. In a remarkable feat of improvisation, Napoleon assembled over 200,000 men in Germany, and with these troops was easily able to hold his own against the roughly similar number of Prussians and Russians available for service against him at this time. Nevertheless, although Alexander and Frederick William were pushed hard, the *grande armée* proved incapable of following up its success – the tens of thousands of horses lost in Russia meant that there were too few cavalry; the raw conscripts who had been called up to fill the ranks were too young to withstand the rigours of the campaign; and the French generals were manifestly past their best. As a result, the Russians and Prussians survived, the emperor letting them off the hook by the offer of a temporary suspension of hostilities known as the armistice of Pläswitz (4 June to 13 August 1813).

We now come to the turning point of the campaign, for the armistice ended with Austria entering the war. Despite having broken with Napoleon, the Austrian chancellor, Metternich, was desperate to maintain a balance between France and Russia, and terrified of the nationalistic effervescence that Stein and his adherents were attempting to provoke across the whole of central Europe. With his best hope a compromise peace, Metternich therefore ignored the generous terms he was offered by Alexander to persuade him to enter the war, and proffered Austria's services as a mediator while at the same time trying (unsuccessfully) to build a neutral bloc among the states of southern Germany. Ratified in the convention of Reichenbach (Dzierzoniow) of 27 June, the result of his discussions with the Allies was that, unless Napoleon agreed to surrender the Illyrian provinces to Austria, recognise the independence of the states of the Confederation of the Rhine, evacuate Germany, return the territories taken from Prussia in 1806 and dissolve the Grand Duchy of Warsaw, Austria would enter the war. Confronted with these terms, Napoleon swore that he would fight on. Nevertheless, eager to win time to bring up the largest possible number of reinforcements and improve the training of his inexperienced forces, the emperor did agree to take part in a conference at Prague. However, even when the Chancellor offered to waive Austria's claim to the Illyrian provinces, it soon became clear that Napoleon had no intention of giving way, and on 12 August Metternich was therefore forced to declare war.

Confronted by the odds he now faced, even Napoleon was hard put to survive. Counting the troops of his remaining allies, he could muster some 335,000 men. However, facing him were a minimum of 515,000 Allies. Dividing his forces so that he could strike out in several directions at once, he succeeded for a short period in staving off disaster, but by mid-October the Allies had effectively surrounded him at Leipzig. There followed the largest, bloodiest and most dramatic battle of the Napoleonic Wars, with the 177,000-strong *grande armée* facing an initial total of over 250,000 Allies. On 16 October simultaneous attacks from north and south were successfully repulsed. At this point Napoleon might yet have got away to the west, but he was expecting 14,000 fresh troops to arrive the following day, and decided to stay put in the expectation that he could secure a genuine victory. In fact, 17 October proved quiet as the Allies were waiting for

140,000 reinforcements of their own, but the following day 300,000 men were launched against the French from all sides. Thanks to Allied bungling and irresolution, the *grande armée* held its ground, but its position was clearly not going to be tenable for very much longer, and in consequence Napoleon ordered a withdrawal. With the only way out of the trap a long and narrow causeway across a marshy river valley, this was an extremely dangerous manoeuvre, but at first all went well: disorganised and exhausted, the Allies did not react until the retreat had been underway for many hours, and even then they were held at bay by the French rearguard. Many of Napoleon's troops therefore escaped, and even more would have done so but for the fact that the causeway was mistakenly blown up. As a result, what could have been a skilful end to an unfortunate campaign was converted into catastrophe, at least 30,000 French troops who might have got away being either killed or captured. Added to the 38,000 casualties the French had suffered over the previous three days, not to mention the many thousands who had been lost earlier in the campaign, this was a blow from which recovery was simply impossible.

Allied casualties had also been very high, but Napoleonic control of central and northern Europe now evaporated overnight. With the *grande armée* fleeing for the Rhine, Napoleon's German satellites either hastily came over to the Allies or collapsed. Holland was also lost at this time, evacuated by the French in the first week of November, and Denmark, which was invaded by Sweden and forced to make peace in January 1814.

Beside events of this magnitude, the incidents of the Peninsular War seem small beer indeed, and all the more so as they had little effect on circumstances in central Europe: *pace* the standard British version, Wellington's victories had little effect on the Austrian decision to enter the war, while a French victory at Leipzig would without doubt have soon been followed by an onslaught of a sort that the Allies would have had little chance of checking. That said, however, the successes of the Anglo-Portuguese armies were considerable. Disagreements with the Spaniards and the social and economic disruption caused by the war prevented Wellington from getting the assistance he had sought from the Spanish armies, but a combination of the operations of the guerrillas of Navarre and the Basque provinces and the interference of Napoleon allowed the British commander to mount an offensive that culminated in a major victory at Vitoria on 21 June. Already a fiction, the French Kingdom of Spain now collapsed altogether: Joseph Bonaparte fled to France, and, while fighting raged in the Pyrenees until the autumn, by the end of the year all that remained to the French was the northern part of Catalonia. Indeed, Wellington had even entered France, having secured a small lodgement in the vicinity of Bayonne. Deciding that the moment was ripe to cut his losses, Napoleon responded by offering to release the imprisoned Ferdinand VII on the understanding that he would make peace with France and expel the Anglo-Portuguese, only to have his terms firmly rejected. Early in 1814 Napoleon decided to release Ferdinand anyway, but, while chaos ensued – in brief the result was a military coup that restored absolutism – it was much too late to make any difference.

By the time Ferdinand got back to Spain in March 1814, Napoleon was on his last legs. Even in the aftermath of Leipzig, Metternich had still been proffering terms – the so-called Frankfurt proposals – that might just have secured France the natural frontiers, but the emperor chose to fight on, the result being that France was now threatened with invasion. It is true that in northern Italy Napoleon's stepson, Eugène de Beauharnais, was holding his own, despite having been driven from the Illyrian provinces by the Austrians and attacked in the rear by a Murat desperate to save his throne. However, in France there were only 85,000 men to defend the eastern frontier against an initial 350,000 Allies, while another 40,000 Frenchmen were facing 90,000 British, Portuguese and Spaniards in the south-west, the bulk of the troops being composed of raw recruits, invalids, customs guards, sailors and gendarmes. Also lacking were arms, uniforms and equipment of all sorts, while many of the marshals were now begging Napoleon to make peace on whatever terms he could get.

Instead of listening to such advice, Napoleon sought rather to improve his bargaining position. Striking hard and fast at a succession of Allied commanders as they invaded eastern France, he secured such a string of victories that it seemed he might have succeeded, the shaken Allies offering peace on the basis of the frontiers of 1792. However, once again Napoleon had been too successful for his own good, elect-ing to fight on in the hope of forcing the resurrection of the Frankfurt proposals. It was his last mistake: though his improvised armies had performed prodigies of valour, little more could be expected of them. As for France, even the few enthusiasts for Jacobinism who still remained were not taken in by attempts to recall 1793, while the bulk of the population was desperate for peace, furiously hostile

71

to the demands of the regime for yet more men, and angry at the depredations of the half-starved French army. Nor were the *notables* any more enthusiastic, the result being that, despite a few instances of guerrilla resistance, expressions of support for the Bourbons began to multiply dramatically. Last but not least, Napoleon's intransigence had driven the Allies closer together, an agreement reached on 1 March 1814 committing all the powers to fight on until the emperor had been defeated.

With matters in such a state, the end came quickly. Though Napoleon continued to fight and manoeuvre relentlessly, he could achieve little. Meanwhile, on 12 March Bordeaux had proclaimed Louis XVIII, its authorities having first made sure that they would immediately be relieved by the Anglo-Portuguese army. At this point the army finally broke as well: mutiny and desertion were now rife; at Lyons, Augereau simply abandoned his headquarters; and in Paris, Marmont first surrendered the city and then led his troops over to the enemy. With Alexander I and Frederick William III both in the capital, the initiative was now seized by the erstwhile foreign minister Talleyrand, who had been living there in semi-retirement and now set about persuading the Allied monarchs that Napoleon had to go. Though the hand of a rather doubtful Alexander (who hated the Bourbons) had to be forced by some hastily organised demonstrations of support for Louis XVIII, on 1 April the Allied monarchs issued a declaration that they would no longer treat with Napoleon or any of his family, and that, insofar as France's future government was concerned, they would respect the wishes of the French people as expressed by an immediate meeting of the Senate. Stage-managed by Talleyrand, this event could have but one end: on 2 April the Senate proclaimed Napoleon to be deposed and formally invited Louis XVIII to return to France.

Meanwhile, Napoleon was at Fontainebleau with 60,000 men. Though the emperor was still ready to fight on, his remaining commanders could take no more, and on 4 April Napoleon was bluntly informed that he must abdicate. The war was not quite over – if only because news of the armistice reached him too late, Wellington had to fight one last battle at Toulouse on 10 April, while various isolated garrisons also held on for some time – but on 28 April Napoleon set sail for the Elban exile that was decreed to be his fate.

So what, then, finally brought down Napoleon? Certainly not some mythical 'people's war', or even a general decision to employ the weapons of the French Revolution against him. The answer, of course, is to be found in Napoleon himself. Tired, ill and increasingly living in a world of fantasy, he threw away his only hope of victory in Russia, and then proceeded repeatedly to reject peace offers that would have left him ruler of an enlarged country. In the process, meanwhile, he made demands on France of a sort which domination of ever greater areas of the Continent had shielded her from since 1799, if not 1793, and thereby shattered the acquiescence – often grudging – with which his rule had hitherto been accepted, while at the same time betraying the interests of the propertied elements that were the real bedrock of his rule. Whatever the reason, the Napoleonic imperium was no more.

Time chart 7: 1815

1815

February	Napoleon sails from Elba.
March	Napoleon overthrows Louis XVIII and is declared an outlaw by the Congress of Vienna; Murat declares for Napoleon.
May	Murat defeated at Tolentino.
June	Napoleon invades Belgium, but is defeated at Waterloo.
June–July	Allies invade France; Napoleon abdicates, surrenders to the British and is dispatched to Saint Helena.
August–September	Last Bonapartist garrisons capitulate; the French Wars are at an end.

7

The War of the Seventh Coalition

In April 1814, Europe could at last relax (or so it seemed): Napoleon appeared to be finished. Resourceful to the end, however, within a few short months the emperor was not only back in Paris, but challenging the judgment of 1814. Yet it was not to be: distrust each other though they did, Britain, Prussia, Austria and Russia feared Napoleon even more. No matter how many victories he succeeded in winning, then, the emperor must ultimately have been overwhelmed. Fortunately for Europe, however, the end came sooner rather than later: thwarted in his efforts to win a great victory at the outset of the campaign, Napoleon was brought to bay and beaten so thoroughly that even he had to concede that there was no other option but surrender.

Worried though some of the Allied statesmen were as to what Napoleon might yet do, in 1814 the victors' attention was rather concentrated on the peace settlement. Insofar as this was concerned, there was little agreement between the powers. It is true that some basic principles – the transfer of Norway to Sweden, the restoration of Austria and Prussia to a position equivalent to that which they had enjoyed prior to Austerlitz and Jena, the retention of a modified version of the Napoleonic state system in Germany, the return of the Bourbons to the throne of Spain, the prevention of further French aggression – had been settled, but many issues had been left unresolved, while much of the detail even of this programme remained vague in the extreme.

With Napoleon defeated, however, the first priority was to come to some agreement about France. In this respect, as we have seen, Louis XVIII had been restored and Napoleon sent to Elba (he was awarded the island in perpetuity, along with a miniscule army, a single frigate and an annual income of 2 million francs), but there yet remained the question of France's borders. As with Napoleon, the path chosen was one of magnanimity. Thus, the treaty of Paris essentially restored the frontiers of 1 November 1792, while awarding Tobago, St Lucia and Mauritius to Britain and St Domingue to Spain. There was, however, no indemnity and no army of occupation, while no attempt was made to restore Europe's looted art treasures to their previous owners, the victors being anxious not to destabilise the Bourbon monarchy. In short, France had got off extraordinarily lightly.

There yet remained the rest of Europe, to discuss which subject a great congress was organised in Vienna in September 1814. No sooner had this opened, however, than the deep-seated tensions that beset the alliance became all too apparent. In brief, the problem centred on the linked questions of Poland and Saxony. Motivated by a bizarre mixture of greed and idealism, Alexander I was proposing the restoration of Poland – interpreted as the Napoleonic Grand Duchy of Warsaw – in the guise of a Russian satellite state ruled by a Romanov prince and provided with a liberal constitution. However, neither Britain, Austria nor Prussia could agree to this, Britain because it would have left Russia far too strong; Austria because it would have left Russia far too strong, handed Prussia enormous gains in Germany as compensation, and stimulated Polish resentment elsewhere; and Prussia because she would have been left with an indefensible eastern frontier (in particular, she wished to regain the fortresses of Thorn (Torun) and Posen (Poznan)). Months of argument ensued, but by the end of 1814 a variety of factors – Russian concessions and suspicion of the British – had caused the Prussians to join the Russians, while Britain, Austria, and a France that had exploited the tension in Vienna to talk her way back into the dealings of the great powers, were united in opposing them. Chiefly at stake was the fate of Saxony, which was exceedingly rich and populous, contiguous to Prussia, under Allied administration thanks to her failure to abandon Napoleon in 1813 while there was still time, and in consequence ideally suited to compensate Prussia for her Polish losses. For a brief moment it seemed that war might follow, but almost immediately Alexander backed off, the fact being that he had no stomach for a resumption of hostilities. Very soon, indeed, a compromise had been agreed whereby most of the Grand Duchy of Warsaw was reconstituted as 'Congress Poland', and Prussia awarded Thorn, Posen and some two-fifths of Saxony.

With Poland and Saxony out of the way, the Congress was able to proceed with other business. Thus, Belgium was joined with Holland in a new Kingdom of the United Netherlands (although the latter had to cede the Cape of Good Hope to Britain); the Rhineland split between Prussia and Bavaria; Genoa added to a restored Piedmont; the Papal States given back to the pope; and Hanover, Oldenburg, Parma, Modena and Tuscany restored as independent states. Meanwhile, Austria acquired Venetia, as well as recovering Lombardy, the Illyrian provinces, Vorarlberg, the Tyrol, Salzburg and Tarnopol; Bavaria acquired Wurzburg and Frankfurt; and Hesse and Prussia acquired what remained of Westphalia. Thus far, meanwhile, Naples had continued to be ruled by Joachim Murat, but Louis XVIII had from the start been anxious to remove him in favour of the exiled Ferdinand IV, the result being that Metternich agreed to send an Austrian army against him in exchange for French support against Russia.

While the map was thus being redrawn, Germany was in the grip of a major reorganisation. The Holy Roman Empire had gone for ever, but the need for the new Germany to be able to defend herself against French aggression dictated the adoption of some form of federal structure. A special committee was established to consider the matter, and a wide variety of schemes was soon under discussion. Hardly had they been tabled, indeed, than they were lent extra point: on 7 March 1815, the stunning news arrived that Napoleon had escaped from Elba.

What had happened? In brief, Napoleon had arrived in his new domain on 4 May 1814. Much cast down, he had initially appeared to accept his new role with equanimity, but it was not long before problems emerged. With incredible stupidity, Louis XVIII not only failed to pay Napoleon's annuity, but also confiscated his considerable personal fortune. At the same time, stories were circulating that plans were afoot to transfer the fallen ruler to a more remote place of incarceration or even to have him murdered. With the Napoleonic administration inevitably pressing ever harder on the population, there was even the danger of revolt. Yet would Napoleon have remained quiet even had all been well? The answer, one suspects, is 'No'. According to all accounts, the emperor had rapidly become bored and restless, while it seems that right from the very beginning he was secretly harbouring dreams of a triumphant return to France.

If this was the case, he can only have been encouraged by the growing evidence that Bourbon rule was proving most unpopular. In the first place, much of the army had not shared the miseries of 1814, the many thousands of men tied up in isolated garrisons that had held out to the end having come home convinced they were undefeated. Sharing their sense of betrayal, meanwhile, were the many prisoners of war who now returned from a captivity that had frequently been quite appalling. Whether they had been held in Allied prisons, manned the walls of such fortresses as Hamburg or fought to defend France herself, many veterans now found themselves homeless and unemployed, while they were joined in misery by at least 20,000 officers who had been stripped of their posts and placed on half pay. Meanwhile, even those officers and men fortunate enough to have secured a place in the new army had to suffer the humiliation of watching hundreds of Bourbon favourites being promoted and decorated.

If veterans of the *grande armée* were prominent in the general grumbling, they were by no means alone. Thus, whereas in 1814 the Bourbons had not appeared so bad an option, perceptions had now changed. In contrast to the moderate views espoused by Louis XVIII in 1813, the *notables* found themselves threatened with loss of influence and land alike: not only were many officials sacked, but alarming rumours began to circulate with regard to the *biens nationaux*. With the regime clearly favouring the nobility, moreover, the principle of the career open to talent also seemed at risk, while still further discontent was aroused by signs of renewed clerical influence. Nor did such policies do anything to reassure committed liberals, this group having already been alienated by the defects of the constitution drawn up by the Senate in April 1814. Lower down the social scale, the peasantry, too, were concerned for any land they had acquired during the Revolution, as well as being rife with rumours that the tithes and feudal dues were to be restored. Finally, assailed by post-war depression and an influx of cheap British goods, the urban workers were suffering severe unemployment, and in consequence regretted the paternalism that had, however imperfectly, shielded them under the empire.

Encouraging as all this was, by February 1815 Napoleon had resolved to escape, and all the more so as the unity of the erstwhile Coalition still seemed decidedly shaky. Viewed in objective terms, the chances of success were slim – so much so, in fact, that it has been claimed that the whole adventure was provoked in an attempt to generate a pretext for 'the monster' to be chained up in some place of exile far from Europe – but on 26 February Napoleon sailed from Elba with his entire army of 750 men. Landing on 1 March near Fréjus, he was soon on the march for Paris. Such troops as were dispatched against him quickly changed sides, and, with Louis XVIII fleeing for the Belgian border, by 20 March the emperor was once again in the capital. No sooner had he arrived than he issued a series of decrees that were designed both to win over the bourgeoisie and appease the populace. Thus, all feudal titles were abolished, the lands of all *émigrés* were expropriated, the press freed from most restraints and major schemes of public works initiated, while the old 'colleges' that had elected the Napoleonic legislature were summoned to a rally in Paris with the express task of approving reforms in the imperial constitution. At the same time, every effort was made to portray the new regime as one of peace, the emperor publicly scoffing at the idea of war and sending ambassadors to Vienna to plead his cause.

Within a very short time, however, a number of things had become apparent. The first was that war was inevitable: hardly had the Allies heard that Napoleon had escaped than they mobilised their armies, declared him to be an outlaw, established a Seventh Coalition and pledged themselves to wage war on the emperor until he was finally overthrown. The second was that Napoleon's efforts to secure general support had fallen on deaf ears. A number of senior dignitaries of the empire had rallied to him, but otherwise the response was distinctly muted. The new constitution was generally scorned by the intelligentsia, for example, while the popular militias – the so-called *fédérés* – that began to appear in the cities and other large towns with the aim of fighting royalism failed to reach out beyond the urban poor and petty bourgeoisie and showed signs of considerable ambivalence towards the regime.

In short, Napoleon was soon in desperate trouble. Determined to raise a large army, he could no longer rely on the acquiescence that had permitted the success of the levies of earlier years. On the contrary, in most parts of France the *notables* who formed the backbone of local government proved singularly uncooperative in the implementation of taxation and conscription alike. Faced by this situation, the Minister of the Interior, Lazare Carnot – the 'architect of victory' of 1793 – dismissed a large number of officials and attempted to replace them with men who were loyal to the regime, only to find that he could obtain few reliable alternatives. As for the lower classes, reports came from large parts of the country of rioting and draft evasion, while the Vendée erupted in fresh revolt.

In these circumstances, it was amazing that Napoleon succeeded in raising a fresh army at all, but, for many veterans of the *grande armée*, the eagles continued to represent the only life they knew. At the same time, the *fédérés* were enough of a threat to scare the propertied classes into at the very least contributing to the war effort on a financial basis, while there were parts of France where conscription was more tolerated than in others. In consequence, by early June at least 280,000 regular troops were available for service, while a month or two more would suffice to bring in the first of the conscripts of 1815 (these forces could be supplemented by a certain number of National Guards, but such was the general discontent that this force had in effect to be discounted). What is more, many were hardened veterans who were as devoted to the emperor as they were enthusiastic about his return.

At the very least, then, Napoleon was in a position to put up a fight, and all the more so as relatively few Allied troops were ready to take the field. His best chance being a dramatic blow that might shatter his enemies' resolve, the emperor immediately struck at the Anglo-Dutch-German army of the Duke of Wellington and the Prussian army of Field Marshal Blücher, both of which were cantoned in southern Belgium. It was an astute choice. Relations between the two were distinctly poor for there had been bitter quarrels as to who should take command of the various German contingents that had been sent to Belgium, and the quality of neither was especially good. Even Wellington's British troops were largely composed of raw recruits, while his Dutch, Belgians and Germans were for the most part singularly unenthusiastic; as for Blücher, he was having to contend with wholesale disaffection among the many Saxon regiments that had been forcibly incorporated into the Prussian ranks.

By early June, then, Napoleon was concentrating as many troops as he dared on the Belgian frontier, his plan being to get between Wellington and Blücher, force them apart, and then defeat them in isolation from one another. However, the first shots of the War of the Seventh Coalition were not in fact those fired by his troops as they streamed across the Belgian frontier south of Charleroi on 15 June. On the contrary, hearing of Metternich's plan to depose him, Murat had mobilised his army, proclaimed a war of Italian liberation and marched north to attack the Austrians, only to be beaten at Tolentino on 1–2 May and forced to flee into exile in France. Needless to say, however, it was in Belgium that the campaign was to be decided.

No sooner had the fighting begun than the emptiness of the emperor's dreams was cruelly revealed. Despite a series of extra-ordinary mistakes on the part of Wellington, Napoleon failed decisively to defeat either of the two armies facing him on 16 June in the twin battles of Ligny and Quatre Bras, this being in the first instance the result of faulty staff work and blunders on the part of the commander of the French left wing, Marshal Ney. Yet Napoleon himself cannot be exonerated for this situation: hampered though he was by the death or absence of many of his best commanders, the emperor is still generally considered to have made some very curious appointments with respect to the army that invaded Belgium.

After 16 June, the French army's situation grew even worse, despite the fact that the Prussians had been badly shaken. Thanks to a series of misconceptions – and possibly a renewed bout of ill-health on the part of Napoleon – the French failed to follow up such advantages as they had gained, and allowed the two Allied armies to retreat towards Brussels on parallel roads that took them to Waterloo and Wavre. Reaching Waterloo, or rather a prominent ridge known as Mont Saint Jean that crossed the Brussels–Charleroi highway at right-angles two miles to the south, Wellington turned to fight, and thus the stage was set for one of the most famous battles of all history.

If Wellington had made serious mistakes at the beginning of the campaign, he more than made up for them now. Conscious of the many deficiencies of his troops, the position he took up was extremely strong and well chosen. Meanwhile, one-third of the army having been detailed to follow Blücher under Marshal Grouchy, the emperor had only 72,000 men to Wellington's 67,000. That said, something might still have been achieved; Napoleon's army was of far higher calibre than Wellington's while it also had far more cannon. However, four factors prevented the tactical victory that was all that was on offer. In the first place, torrential rain had so soaked the battlefield that the first attacks had to be delayed until nearly midday; in the second, the resistance put up by Wellington's army was much greater than might have been expected; in the third, there were serious mistakes in the handling of the French attacks; and in the fourth, Grouchy failed either to stop Blücher from joining Wellington, or to march to Napoleon's support. As a result, by the time the French finally broke into Wellington's centre at around six o'clock in the evening, large numbers of Prussians were assailing their right flank. In desperation, the emperor now committed part of the infantry of the Imperial Guard, only for them to be thrown back in disorder. It was the end. Utterly exhausted, under heavy fire and unsettled by rumours of treason, the French army disintegrated, while Wellington ordered a general advance. With the Prussians pressing in on their flank and rear, Napoleon's forces were soon jammed together in a panic-stricken flight along the main road. Pursued for miles by Allied cavalry, they left behind them 25,000 casualties, though at 21,000, Allied losses numbered only slightly fewer. As Blücher famously remarked to Wellington when they encountered one another, 'Quelle affaire!'

What an affair, indeed. For Napoleon, all hope was gone. There were still plenty of troops available, but it was quite plain that neither the *notables* nor the peasantry would accept further fighting. In a rare moment of realism, on 22 June the emperor therefore abdicated for a second time. There followed several weeks of confusion in which neither Napoleon nor the provisional government that had been formed in Paris seem to have known what to do for the best, but on 15 July the emperor finally surrendered to the British at Rochefort. Far to the east, meanwhile, six Allied armies had been pouring over the frontier in the face of scattered resistance. Desperate to end the fighting, the provisional government sued for peace, but the Allies insisted on pressing on until they had captured Paris, which fell on 7 July. A few die-hard garrisons held on into the summer – the very last, Montmédy, did not surrender until 13 September – but the French Wars were finally at an end.

There is little left to tell. Undisturbed by the return of Napoleon, the process of peacemaking went on in Vienna, the most important item of business resolved at this time being the shape that was to be given to the new Germany (in brief, it was decided that the German states would be united in a loose confederation), and on 9 June 1815 the final act of agreement was ratified by all the powers involved in the Congress. Napoleon was sent to end his days on distant St Helena, and a France once again ruled by Louis XVIII was forced to accept a new peace settlement which stripped her of a number of strategic frontier districts – the general frontier adopted was now that of 1790 – enforced the return of many art objects, imposed an indemnity of 700 million francs, and subjected her to military occupation. As for the great powers, on 20 November 1815 Britain, Russia, Prussia and Austria entered into the so-called Quadruple Alliance, whereby they engaged both to keep the peace against France and hold regular congresses to ensure that war did not break out again. Prior to that, Russia, Prussia and Austria had signed the much-misunderstood Holy Alliance, the point of this agreement being not so much to crush revolution wherever it raised its head, but to promote international stability.

Much criticised though it has often been, the peace settlement that resulted from the French Wars was by no means the disaster of legend. No attempt was made to turn the clock back to 1789, and, if many territorial changes were made, few were especially objectionable to the populations concerned, among whom nationalism had acquired little real purchase. At the same time, too, the new frontiers were on the whole eminently justifiable, the Europe that emerged from Vienna being, as Paul Schroeder in particular has argued, far more stable than that of 1918 or 1945, let alone than those of earlier general peace settlements. If so, this was no mere accident: as a number of figures had recognised over the past twenty-three years, the powers of Europe could no longer engage in the endless dynastic warfare of the eighteenth century, for the stakes were too high and the costs too great. The watchword of the Congress, in fact, was not reaction but rather peace, and, in the wake of the seven million deaths that seem a reasonable estimate of the total 'blood tax' exacted by the French Wars, one can thank God for it.

How, though, are we to estimate the role of the French Wars in European history? Here again, much of the traditional version of events is open to challenge. To argue, for example, that the period 1792 to 1815 gave birth to an age of liberalism and nationalism is to run the risk of serious exaggeration. That said, however, the French Wars certainly had a considerable impact on the politics of the first half of the nineteenth century, in that officer corps were frequently drawn into the discourse of the day (whether conservative or liberal) and progressive political movements instilled with a warlike ethos which some were not to shake off until the First World War. Also worth mentioning is the impact of the French Wars on the international economy, the dominant centres of trade and manufacture having been forcibly shifted away from the maritime littoral in the direction of new centres of industry in such areas as Saxony and the Ruhr. Most importantly, however, Europe was afforded an era of relative peace which allowed her to give full play to her considerable economic advantages: not for another half century were the powers of Europe willing once more to make use of war as an integral instrument of foreign policy in the style of the eighteenth century.

8

Issues and conclusions

Such, then, is the basic outline of the French Wars. A complex series of struggles in which revolutionary and Napoleonic France was pitted against a series of transient (at least, until the very end) and ever-changing coalitions of the other European powers, they completely failed to follow the pattern of 'the French against the rest' that might have been expected had the French Revolution cut across international relations in the way that has often been argued. Had the powers subordinated their every interest to defeating the threat to the old order supposedly thrown up by the events of 1789, or, for that matter, had France devoted herself to revolutionising the entire Continent, life would be very much simpler. However, in neither instance was this the case. On the contrary, Britain, Spain, Prussia, Austria and Russia all continued to pursue traditional foreign policy aims that in many cases did not coincide with the idea of an all-out war against the French. For a long time responses to France therefore included not just armed conflict, but also neutrality, appeasement, co-operation and alliance, while the idea of turning the clock back to 1789 receded ever further into the background, if indeed it was ever there at all. This was never to return: by 1814 there was a general assumption that France would be some sort of constitutional monarchy. Yet in other respects there was a vital change. Little by little, the powers gradually came to the conclusion that the great and overriding issue of the day was France's restriction to a much smaller

84

sphere of influence than that aspired to by either Republic or Empire. In short, the wars did indeed become a case of 'the French against the rest', the result being that Napoleon eventually faced such odds that even he could not prevail.

There is, however, a rival explanation for the course of events. We now come to the question of the transformation in warfare supposedly wrought by the French Revolution. Once the concept of such a transformation has been accepted, France's initial success is easily explained. In brief, the past – the 'cabinet army' of the eighteenth century – met the future – the 'nation in arms' of the nineteenth and twentieth centuries – and was vanquished. With their small professional armies, their mercenary soldiers, their feudal societies, and their authoritarian and unrepresentative political systems, France's opponents could match neither her military capacities nor her commitment to the struggle. However, this situation did not last. Consistently worsted, the powers elected to fight fire with fire by reforming their armies and initiating a variety of political and social reforms. As a result (or so it is claimed), France was confronted with new 'nations-in-arms' at a time when, thanks to Napoleon, she had ceased to be one herself.

The position adopted by this pamphlet with regard to these issues should be clear enough. To what extent, however, do its conclusions mirror the recent historiography of the revolutionary and Napoleonic era? Beginning with the nature of the French Wars, the traditional view is far from dead. That said, though, the old orthodoxy is at its strongest among historians who are French, or at least pro-French. The strongly revisionist François Furet, for example, wrote that 'when war came, it would be a war between two ideas' and that 'even French victories could at best result only in truces; to look for peace was as suspect as being defeated – both were betrayals of revolutionary patriotism' (F. Furet, *The French Revolution, 1770–1814* (Oxford, 1992), pp. 103–5). Implicit in Furet's argument is at least the admission that the war sprang from the Revolution, but other observers may be found who would still argue that, if the war was indeed an ideological one, it was one that France was forced into, and furthermore one in which her every action was dictated by the need to stave off counter-revolution. A good example here is the Marxist historian, Albert Soboul. Thus, in his best-known work, *The French Revolution, 1787–1799* (London, 1974), Soboul argues that France went to war in 1792 because of the counter-revolutionary threat at home and abroad, that the Convention called on the peoples of Europe to revolt as a means of emasculating the *ancien régime*, and that annexation was 'the only possible policy if counter-revolution was to be avoided in the occupied countries' (Vol. I, p. 289). In the case of Britain in particular meanwhile, the political threat was accompanied by an economic one, for Britain's commercial and economic supremacy was being threatened by the growth of France's own trade and industry. As Soboul went on to write:

> The conflict was due in large measure to . . . the commercial, naval and colonial rivalry between France and Britain. . . . The struggle that developed between France and Britain was no longer a war between rival monarchs, but was in many respects a war between nations fighting for mastery in both the political and the economic sphere.
>
> (*The French Revolution*, Vol. I, pp. 290–1)

As far as the period 1792 to 1799 is concerned, then, defence of the idea that the French Wars were an ideological struggle is strongly linked with a position of sympathy with the Revolution, for closely connected with it is the idea that the Wars were also a defensive struggle in which France was sinned against rather than sinning. With the advent of Napoleon, however, matters become more complicated, for many writers who were inclined to defend the actions of the Revolution in the Wars of the First and Second Coalitions were of the view that the Corsican general had overthrown the cause of political and social progress in France, and consequently everything that took place after 1799 was the fruit of vainglory, lust for power and naked aggression. Yet even among historians who are essentially favourable to the French Revolution there are those who believe the ideological and, by implication, essentially defensive, conflict of the 1790s continued after 1799. In some instances the tone is rather grudging – 'After 1795 the French Revolution continued, but wearing a military uniform and without the active support of the masses' (G. Lewis, *The French Revolution: rethinking the debate* (London, 1993), p. 52) – but in others it is positively enthusiastic. Thus, for Jacques Godechot:

> The spread of revolutionary ideas did not end when a military dictator came to power in France in the person of Napoleon Bonaparte. The soldiers of the Consulate and the Empire carried the revolutionary doctrines to regions where they had as yet

hardly penetrated – Hungary, Russia, the south of Spain and
Portugal.

(J. Godechot, *France and the Atlantic Revolution
of the Eighteenth Century, 1770–1799* (London, 1965), p. 6)

Similarly, for Eric Hobsbawm:

The French soldiers who campaigned from Andalusia to Moscow,
from the Baltic to Syria . . . pushed the universality of their revolution home more effectively than anything else could have done.
And the doctrines they carried with them, even under Napoleon . . .
were universal doctrines, as the governments knew, and as the
peoples themselves were soon to know also.

(E. Hobsbawm, *The Age of Revolution, 1789–1848*
(London, 1962), p. 117)

It is not, however, among historians of the French Revolution that
this tendency to identify Napoleon with the French Revolution
and charge the *ancien régime* with all the blame for the slaughter of
the first fifteen years of the nineteenth century is most strongly
entrenched. In both power and exile, Napoleon made the idea that
he was a man of peace and a man of the Revolution the heart of
the campaign of propaganda with which he sought to legitimise his
rule. The resultant Napoleonic legend being a phenomenon of great
power, it has secured the services of a variety of historians ever
since, although they have done little more than embellish and recapi-
tulate the arguments of the source of their inspiration. Summarised
as far as their French representatives are concerned in Pieter Geyl's
masterly *Napoleon, For and Against* (London, 1949), this school of
thought is most accessibly expressed in Vincent Cronin's *Napoleon*
(London, 1971). Little more than an exercise in hagiography, this
work presents us with a Napoleon who was over and over again
forced into war against his will, who only intervened in Spain out of
a quixotic desire to extend the benefits of liberty, equality and frater-
nity to her people, and who rejected the successive peace terms that he
was offered in 1813–14 out of patriotism. Thus:

Napoleon . . . saw the empire, a new order embodying the rights of
man, challenged by the old order, embodying privilege and faded
glories. . . . Napoleon saw the empire also as the embodiment of
France's glory. French ideas, French lives, French toil had built

the empire up. It therefore became a point of honour for France and for himself, the elected ruler of France, to defend the empire. . . . So though he needed peace, Napoleon believed that it would be wrong to make peace at any price.

(Napoleon, p. 425)

What, then, of the charge of personal ambition? Napoleon is certainly recognised as a man of 'inflexible will', but this characteristic, it seems, 'could never have stemmed from so feeble a thing as personal ambition; it was rooted in the principles of the French Revolution' (*Napoleon*, p. 428). Also important, according to Cronin, was honour – 'Honour, not ambition or war, was what Napoleon really valued most in the world. Honour to him was like a sword blade, and love of honour like a kiss on the naked steel' (ibid.).

If only he could have had 'peace with honour', concludes Cronin, Napoleon could have been happy, but 'peace with honour' was not available, and therefore he fought on. Fortunately for the student, however, such ideas have not been allowed to go unchallenged. Returning to the subject of the French Wars as a whole, the historiography of the period has been immeasurably enriched by the publication of Paul Schroeder's *The Transformation of European Politics, 1763–1848* (Oxford, 1994). A massive work of great scholarship, this inevitably has the French Wars at its very heart, but the picture it presents is far removed from the simplicities of arguments based on ideological struggle. Even if he ultimately remained loyal to his essentially political convictions, Soboul was too honest a historian entirely to ignore the problems that beset the 'French versus the rest' school of thought, specifically noting the multiple rivalries and differences that divided France's enemies from one another. Schroeder, however, places these difficulties centre stage, and in the process shows that the conduct of international diplomacy continued to be governed by more or less traditional considerations for many years after 1792, while at the same time demonstrating that responses to France in the period 1790 to 1796, in particular, were closely bound up with events in Poland and the Balkans. At the time that Schroeder was writing, Tim Blanning had already published his study *The Origins of the French Revolutionary Wars* (London, 1986). This suggested that Europe did not slide into war on account of an irreconcilable ideological divide, but rather as a result of political manoeuvring in France and general muddle and misconception. Immediately after the publication of *The Transformation of European Politics*, Blanning added to the debate with a second work which argued, as Schroeder had done, that the French Wars were in fact but one part of a general crisis in international relations that would have exploded in the last years of the eighteenth century even had there been no revolution in France whatsoever. Hence his at first sight somewhat eccentric decision to date them from 1787 (cf. T. Blanning, *The French Revolutionary Wars, 1787–1792* (London, 1996)).

Both Schroeder and Blanning are strongly revisionist historians who are inclined to be sceptical with regard to what Norman Hampson has called 'the old myth that there was a French Revolution that was by definition a boon to humanity in general' (in G. Best (ed.), *The Permanent Revolution: the French Revolution and its legacy, 1789–1989* (London, 1988), p. 232). However, their views are in some respects shared even by historians of whose work this cannot be said. For Alan Forrest, for example, the wars of 1792 to 1801 started off as a Brissotin scheme to win power and, as a necessary concomitant, transform France into a Republic, and then degenerated into a war of conquest that 'took much of the idealism out of the Revolution' (A. Forrest, *The French Revolution* (Oxford, 1995), pp. 110–32). Space here might also be found for Michael Sydenham, who, while maintaining that 'the causes of this constant conflict are . . . so complex that it would be manifestly unjust to hold the French . . . wholly responsible for it', was forced to recognise that 'the republicans refused to recognise the validity of international law or of their neighbours' rights' (M. Sydenham, *The First French Republic, 1792–1804* (London, 1974), p. 304). In the same way, meanwhile, in writing about the general fear provoked by France in the 1790s, William Doyle has to admit that this did not really gather pace until after general war had broken out, that there was little will for war with France prior to 1792, and that it was French aggression, or, at least, the revolutionaries' tendency to 'seek to solve their problems by inflicting them on their neighbours', that gave birth to the constellation of enemies with which the Revolution was eventually presented (W. Doyle, *The Oxford History of the French Revolution* (Oxford, 1989), pp. 173–219 *passim*).

Ideological conflict was certainly present, then, but it at best nurtured the wars rather than actually giving birth to them. Even this nuance is absent from most recent writing on Napoleon, however. Thus, if we take the vital work of the highly influential and strongly Marxist Georges Lefebvre as a starting point, we find that the French ruler's own actions are not only placed at the very centre of the

Napoleonic Wars, but are suggested as their root cause. Lefebvre cannot resist the notion that Britain and France were locked in perpetual economic and commercial rivalry and conflict, but, even so, he sees the emperor as having become 'stupefied with his own omnipotence and . . . infatuated with his own omniscience', remarking, 'That is why it is idle to seek for limits to Napoleon's policy, or for a final goal at which he would have stopped', and, still more bluntly, 'Bonaparte was simply not interested in keeping the peace' (G. Lefebvre, *Napoleon: from 18 Brumaire to Tilsit, 1799–1807* (New York, 1969), pp. 63–7 *passim*). Strenuous in his denial of the idea that the emperor was a man of the Revolution, his conclusion is emphatic. Thus:

> It would seem at least probable that the annexation of Belgium and the left bank of the Rhine would expose France to new attacks. But . . . the best means of defending the natural frontiers was not . . . expanding beyond them and so giving rise to coalitions in self-defence. Yet this was what Napoleon was personally responsible for setting in train.
> (G. Lefebvre, *Napoleon: from Tilsit to Waterloo, 1807–1815* (New York, 1969), pp. 368–9)

Broadly speaking, this is the line that has been taken by most academic historians in Britain and the United States ever since. For Schroeder, for example, Napoleon is little more than an unprincipled adventurer with a 'criminal' foreign policy, while recent years have seen the publication of a series of works that have strongly distanced themselves from Bonapartist fantasies. Setting aside my own *Wars of Napoleon* (London, 1995), examples, however nuanced, include Michael Broers' *Europe under Napoleon, 1799–1815* (London, 1996), Martin Lyons' *Napoleon Bonaparte and the Legacy of the French Revolution* (London, 1994) and Geoffrey Ellis' *Napoleon* (London, 1997). Sydenham, too, stressed the role of Napoleon in both perpetuating and precipitating conflict in the period from 1796 to 1803, while even popular biography seems to have turned against the emperor, the latest two examples of the genre – Alan Schom's *Napoleon Bonaparte* (New York, 1997) and Frank McLynn's *Napoleon: a biography* (London, 1997) – having both been more or less critical in their approach. Finally, for a French example, one may turn to Jean Tulard's *Napoleon: the myth of the saviour* (London, 1984).

While dissenting voices may yet be found – one such is Furet, whose decision to end his *French Revolution* not in 1799 but in 1814 symbolises both a continued identification of Napoleon with the Revolution and an assumption that he was indeed faced by a counter-revolutionary crusade – the general pattern of the current historiography with regard to the nature of the French Wars is therefore clear. What, though, about the manner in which they were fought and ultimately won? Traditional interpretations of this question that can be used as a starting point for wider reading are to be found in G. Best, *War and Society in Revolutionary Europe, 1770–1870* (London, 1982), and G. Rothenburg, *The Art of War in the Age of Napoleon* (London, 1977). Works that include a more detailed exposition of particular aspects of 'revolutionary' explanations for the French triumph include B. Nosworthy, *With Musket, Cannon and Sword: battle tactics of Napoleon and his enemies* (New York, 1996), J. Lynn, *Bayonets of the Republic: motivation and tactics in the army of revolutionary France, 1791–1794* (Urbana, Illinois, 1984), and J. Bertaud, *The Army of the French Revolution: from citizen soldiers to instrument of power* (Princeton, 1988).

Here too, however, debate has moved on. French military performance in general, and the solidity of the nation-in-arms in particular, have been called into question by a variety of works including Alan Forrest's *Conscripts and Deserters: the army and French society during the revolution and empire* (Oxford, 1989) and Paddy Griffith's *Art of War of Revolutionary France, 1789–1802* (London, 1998). Also worthy of notice here is Blanning's *French Revolutionary Wars*, for, while accepting that the Revolution did throw up a number of undeniable military advantages – most particularly, greater numbers and a more aggressive style of waging war – Blanning points out that the despised cabinet armies remained able to hold their own except when heavily outnumbered or confronted by the genius of Napoleon Bonaparte. As for the idea that the French were eventually overthrown by making use of the same military and political methods that had supposedly brought them to power, this has been subjected to serious question. In *The Spanish Army in the Peninsular War* (Manchester, 1988), for example, I have suggested that limits can be found to popular enthusiasm for war against the French even in the context of the most famous and most genuine example of an attempt to mobilise an entire populace in an anti-Napoleonic crusade. However, by far the most comprehensive demolition job in this respect has been performed in the case of Germany and, more especially, Prussia.

Thus, while not denying that a certain amount of popular enthusiasm could be found in the campaigns of 1813 to 1814, a succession of historians have pointed out the glaring weaknesses in the time-honoured version of events. For Brendan Simms, for example:

> Napoleon was defeated not by the *volk* or the emerging modern society of the Prussian reformers. Rather, Napoleon was beaten by the armies of the *ancien régime*. . . . Even the national character of the war can be disputed. . . . The wars of liberation were at least as much wars of cabinets as they were wars 'of the people'.
>
> (B. Simms, *The Struggle for Mastery in Germany* (London, 1998), pp. 102–3)

Equally, for James Sheehan, 'The *volk*'s role in its own liberation was, at best, a minor one. Napoleon was defeated by regular armies, not patriotic poets and quaintly attired gymnasts' (J. Sheehan, *German History, 1770–1866* (Oxford, 1989), p. 386).

To conclude: academic views on the French Wars are in the midst of a period of reassessment which has seen a steady retreat from old certainties. The process is not yet complete, there still being many areas of Europe about which we do not know enough to be able comfortably to reject historiographical orthodoxy altogether. However, sufficient progress has been made to make it impossible to sustain a view of the conflicts of 1792 to 1815 that sees them primarily in terms of ideological division or seeks a social or political explanation for their course and outcome. The weakness in such broad and confident arguments is their tendency to elide inconvenient details. Like it or not, the study of the French Wars, or, for that matter, any other conflict, demands an acceptance of traditional forms of history that all too often run the risk of being sidelined.

Bibliograpical essay

Let us begin with studies of the revolutionary and Napoleonic period in general. Surprisingly, there appears to be no single-volume study of the whole of the French Wars, but G. Rudé, *Revolutionary Europe, 1783–1815* (London, 1964), is a helpful introduction to the period, while the course of international relations is reviewed with consummate skill in P. Schroeder, *The Transformation of European Politics 1763–1848* (Oxford, 1994). For a detailed military history that covers the main campaigns (but not those in which Napoleon played no part), there is no substitute for D. Chandler, *The Campaigns of Napoleon: the mind and method of history's greatest soldier* (London, 1966). As competition for Chandler, there is the slimmer O. Connelly, *Blundering to Glory: Napoleon's military campaigns* (Wilmington, Delaware, 1987), and G. Rothenberg, *The Napoleonic Wars* (London, 1999), the latter being especially noteworthy for its beautiful maps. Rather broader, geographically speaking, is P. Fregosi, *Dreams of Empire: Napoleon and the First World War, 1792–1815* (London, 1989). Also relevant in this respect, of course, are studies of Napoleon, of which the three most recent examples are G. Ellis, *Napoleon* (London, 1997), F. McLynn, *Napoleon: a biography* (London, 1997), and A. Schom, *Napoleon Bonaparte* (London, 1997).

If there are few general studies of the period, the art of war is well covered. Here mention should be made of G. Rothenberg, *The Art of Warfare in the Age of Napoleon* (London, 1977), G. Nafziger, *Imperial*

Bayonets: tactics of the Napoleonic battery, battalion and brigade as found in contemporary regulations (London, 1996), B. Nosworthy, *With Musket, Cannon and Sword: battle tactics of Napoleon and his enemies* (New York, 1996), and R. Muir, *Tactics and the Experience of Battle in the Age of Napoleon* (London, 1998).

As far as the 1790s are concerned, T. Blanning, *The French Revolutionary Wars, 1787–1802* (London, 1996), is a splendid introduction and particularly useful for sixth-formers and undergraduates, which can usefully be supplemented by Blanning's *Origins of the French Revolutionary Wars* (London, 1986). M. Sydenham, *The First French Republic, 1792–1804* (London, 1974), links domestic politics with international relations in a most helpful fashion, while there is still much to be gained from R. Phipps, *The Armies of the First French Republic and the Rise of the Marshals of Napoleon I* (Oxford, 1926–39). For the army itself, see J. Lynn, *The Bayonets of the Republic: motivation and tactics in the army of revolutionary France, 1791–94* (Urbana, Illinois, 1984), A. Forrest, *The Soldiers of the French Revolution* (Durham, North Carolina, 1989), and J. Bertaud, *The Army of the French Revolution: from citizen soldiers to instrument of power* (Princeton, 1988).

The Napoleonic period has an obvious starting point in the shape of C. Esdaile, *The Wars of Napoleon* (London, 1995), and D. Gates, *The Napoleonic Wars, 1803–1815* (London, 1997), both of which are specifically aimed at the sixth-form and undergraduate market. As for the empire, see S. Woolf, *Napoleon's Integration of Europe* (London, 1991), G. Ellis, *The Napoleonic Empire* (London, 1991), M. Broers, *Europe under Napoleon, 1799–1815* (London, 1996), and M. Lyons, *Napoleon Bonaparte and the Legacy of the French Revolution* (London, 1994). Of these, Ellis's work is by far the most useful for newcomers to the subject, while sixth-formers especially are recommended to look at A. Stiles, *Napoleon, France and Europe* (London, 1993), and D. G. Wright, *Napoleon and Europe* (London, 1984), both of which also contain useful introductions to Napoleon's career as a whole.

Many studies also exist of the various armies that took part in the Napoleonic Wars. In this respect, J. Elting, *Swords around a Throne: Napoleon's grande armée* (New York, 1988), and F. Schneid, *Soldiers of Napoleon's Kingdom of Italy: army, state and society* (Boulder, Colorado, 1995), are helpful on the imperial forces, while some of the armies which they fought are dealt with by C. Esdaile, *The Spanish Army in the Peninsular War* (Manchester, 1988), G. Rothenberg, *Napoleon's Great Adversaries: the Archduke Charles and the Austrian Army, 1792–1814* (London, 1982), W. Shanahan, *Prussian Military Reforms,*

1786–1813 (New York, 1945), and the old but still unequalled C. Oman, *Wellington's Army, 1809–1814* (London, 1913). Finally, for an exciting study of popular resistance whose style ought to have been replicated in other instances, see J. Tone, *The Fatal Knot: the guerrilla war in the defeat of Napoleon in Spain* (Chapel Hill, North Carolina, 1994).